I shall pass through
this world but once.
Any good therefore
that I can do or any
kindness that I can
show to any human
being. let me do it now.
Let me not defer or
neglect it for I shall
not pass this way
again.

EX LIBRIS

HOW TO PLAN AND CONDUCT A
Bicentennial Celebration

Ye Olde Inquirer

PRICE ONLY FIVE COPPERS   *MONDAY*, May 15.   *The 173rd year of our Independence*

Printed by **The Philadelphia Inquirer**
on Broad Street at Callow Hill

PHILADELPHIA, May 15

THIS DAY there gathered on the historic flagstones of Independence Square, in our City, a Concourfe of people to witnefs a fpectacle depicting the adoption of the Declaration of Independence and the proclaiming of Liberty throughout the land.

The *Pageant*, which was greeted with great Rejoicing, launched the 1950 Savings Bonds INDEPENDENCE DRIVE of Thefe United States. The SPECTACLE OF INDEPENDENCE was directed with exceeding Skill by the moft efteemed Adele Gutman Nathan, a Gentlewoman of New York Town, and Blevins Davis, Efq., of Independence, Mo., who were received with great affection by the Multitude affembled.

Maurice Evans, Efq., of public renown for his laudable Thefpian exploits in the works of Shakefpeare and Bernard Shaw, enacted the role of pageant Narrator.

The *Pageant* unfolded fhortly after the noon hour with a Convergence of Bands from Bok Vocational & Technical School, Roman Catholic High School, Northeast High School and the Police and Firemen's Band.

Thereupon the Multitude was enlightened by felicitous addreffes of Welcome by Arthur C. Kaufmann, Efq., Chairman of the Phila. Civic Committee for the Bond Drive, the Hon. Bernard Samuel, Efq., Mayor of our Fair City, Ronald Reagan, Efq., of Hollywood.

Then the Secretary of The Treasury of Thefe United States, John W. Snyder, Efq., addreffed a few words to the affemblage.

At this Juncture, the *Pageant* proper commenced. Authentically Coftumed to reprefent thofe famed Patriots who founded this great Nation on July 4, 1776, public-fpirited Citizens of our City affembled in a fitting tableau, portraying John Hancock, Efq., Thomas Jefferson, Efq., Benjamin Franklin, Efq., and many others. The general public attendant at that Hiftoric time were alfo depicted. Among them were John Dunlap, Efq., the public printer, and the cuftodian-bell-ringer of the State Houfe, Andrew McNair, Efq.

As a fitting climax to the infpired performance, the bell-ringer, McNair, again rang out the glad Tidings of Independence, the rich Peals founding fweet and clear from an exact replica of the Liberty Bell, with the crack omitted, fpecially caft for the event. This replica and the founding of the original Liberty Bell were carried acrofs this great Land over Radio and Televifion.

Thereupon the *Pageant* clofed.

We rejoice in the energy and well-timed exertions of thefe public-fpirited Citizens. The zeal and co-operation difplayed by the Performers and the Multitude deferves our higheft Commendation and Praife, and offers a pleafing proof of the fpirit and alacrity with which our Fellow Citizens are ready to maintain and fupport our Excellent and Profperous Nation.

Washington, D. C. 1950

THE Secretary of the Treafury of Thefe United States, the Hon. John W. Snyder, Efq., by Proclamation:

Refolved: that the *Savings Bonds* INDEPENDENCE DRIVE will be opened at Independence Square, in the "Birthplace of American Liberty," Philadelphia, in the Commonwealth of Pennfylvania on May 15, 1950.

In purfuance of the previous refolution, Citizens are requefted to meet the quota of $653,950,000 in Series "E" Savings Bonds.

The Printers throughout Thefe United States are requefted to infert the above in their papers.

LINEAL DESCENDANTS OF

Signers of Declaration of Independence

Prefent at the impreffive Ceremonies launching the Independence Drive were thirteen Lineal Defcendants of Signers of the Declaration from each of the 13 Original Colonies. The States and Signers reprefented were:

New Hampfhire
Matthew Thornton *by Commdr. Matthew Thornton Betton, USN (ret.) Portfmouth, N. H.*

Maffachufetts
John Adams *by John Quincy Adams, Bofton, Mafs.*

Connecticut
Samuel Huntington & Oliver Wolcott *by Samuel Huntington Wolcott, Bofton, Mafs.*

Rhode Ifland & Providence Plantations
Stephen Hopkins *by Mrs. Everitt St. J. Chaffee, Providence, R. I.*

New York
William Floyd *by William Floyd Haneman, Woodmere, L. I., N. Y.*

New Jerfey
John Hart *by Mrs. James Clark Corson, Paulfboro, N. J.*

Pennfylvania
Benjamin Rush *by Benjamin Rush, Jr., Devon, Penna. (Official hoft to the others)*

Delaware
Thomas McKean *by Mrs. Douns Fisher, Bryn Mawr, Penna.*

Maryland
William Paca *by William Winchester Paca, Jr., Richmond, Va.*

Virginia
Carter Braxton *by Hugh Gwynn Poutles, Arlington, Va.*

North Carolina
John Penn *by Mrs. Robert W. Williams, Arlington, Va.*

South Carolina
Arthur Middleton *by Ann Marsden Smith, Richmond, Va.*

Georgia
There being no living defcendants of its 3 Signers, is reprefented by Henry Norris Platt, Jr., Cheftnut Hill, Penna., a Georgian by defcent and defcendant of Thomas Jefferson of Virginia, author of ye immortal Declaration.

ONE-HORSE GIG
ALSO

A fedan chair, one-horfe gig and broom of Colonial defign were among the many properties deftined to be ufed in the SPECTACLE OF INDEPENDENCE to lend the proper authenticity.

There was widefpread fearch for other exceeding rare Remembrances of the Colonial Days. As a confequence, mufkets, a fword, a gold-headed cane and a cart and donkey were alfo difclofed.

Other neceffities to be obtained were a marionette theatre on wheeled cart, Band inftruments of the period for a "little German Band," flags bearing the flogan "Liberty Or Death," a Coneftoga wagon, a parrot, long loaves of bread and a horfe for Cæsar Rodney.

All thefe articles were unearthed, due to the Untiring and Enterprifing fpirits of all the Committee concerned.

For Savannah (G.)
The Brigantine
GEORGIA PACKET
EDWARD BURROWS, MASTER

is a remarkable faft failer, has good accommodations for paffengers, and will pofitively fail on the 12th inft. For freight or paffage, apply to the faid mafter on board, at Mifflin's wharf between Vine and Race-ftreet.

WORCESTER, June 28, 1776

THE Superior Court of Judicature, of Affize, and General Jail Delivery, fat laft week at Ipfwich, in and for the county of Effex, and tranfacted bufinefs both of a criminal and civil nature, to the great joy and fatisfaction of every true friend to his country, order, and civil fociety, it being the firft under the aufpices of our new government.

Frefh Portugal Lemons

Now Landing on the *St. George*, Capt. Deboffa, from Oporto, in very fine Order. Alfo, very fuperior old Red Port Wine, in pipes, hogfheads & quartercafks—for Sale by

PETER BLIGHT

NOTICE—*All perfons having pawned* goods at No. 280 SOUTH ftreet, are requefted to come and redeem them, at the Pawnbroker has quit the bufinefs.

N.B.—He will attend in the store every day from 9 O'clock until 3 O'clock in the afternoon, Sundays excepted, to deliver the goods.

HOW TO PLAN AND CONDUCT A

Bicentennial Celebration

Adele Gutman Nathan

Illustrated by
Alfred Stern and Ben Edwards

a Giniger/Stackpole Book

STACKPOLE BOOKS

HOW TO PLAN AND CONDUCT A BICENTENNIAL CELEBRATION
Copyright © 1971 by
ADELE GUTMAN NATHAN

Published by
STACKPOLE BOOKS
Cameron and Kelker Streets
Harrisburg, Pa. 17105

ISBN 0-8117-0853-5
Library of Congress Catalog Card Number 70-162446

Printed in U.S.A.

Contents

List of Illustrations and Charts

Acknowledgments

WHEN KEN GINIGER first talked to me about writing this book, I thought it would be an easy job. But I soon found that it is difficult to compress a lifetime of experience into a couple of hundred written pages. I had my lectures at the American Theatre Wing Professional School of the Drama to begin with, but there were also three full-to-bursting files to be sifted in order to authenticate what I wanted to write about. I could never have finished the job without the help of many people, most of whom had worked with me before, in one way or another, and who were ready to come up with their recollections and memorabilia.

Chief among these, of course, is Alfred Stern, who, though now deep in projects of his own, took the time not only to help reconstruct the charts but also to do many illustrations for the book.

Lillian Gainsburgh, my associate for many years, jogged my memory, gave me invaluable editorial help untiringly, and often made me work when I was reluctant to do so.

Ben Edwards, the designer-producer, generously added the illustrations for the section, "Parades."

Ann Ronell, the composer-lyricist, who has created the musical background for many motion pictures, gave most solid suggestions as to the use of music and sound, and a fine bibliography. Dr. Alice Harris of Hofstra University helped with the section on historical background, and Gordon Dodge of Pace College with the technical details. I used the excellent vignettes which Mrs. Roy Gifford created for the Gettysburg Centennial, as my model for the section, "Vignettes." Harold Peterson, Chief Curator of the National Park Service, and well-known authority on the Revolutionary period, put me on the trail of information in many areas; as did Sam Cohen, whose interest in the restoration of the Thomas Jefferson house in Philadelphia made him the possessor of much unusual data.

Janet Finney of Random House, Alice Thorne of Grosset & Dunlap, and Charlotte Seitlin of Simon & Schuster, told me where to find background material. Walter Riemer, Blevins Davis, Ray Middleton, Nannine Joseph, and Vice President C. R. Zarfoos of the B. & O.-C. & O. Railroad, helped by recalling our adventures together.

Designs and drawings in my possession by the late Raymond Sovey, the distinguished theatrical designer, further brought back remembrance of our many successful projects.

Jeanette Longyear researched tirelessly, and Beth Fine and Lillian Gerber helped whip the manuscript into its final shape.

A word of thanks also goes to Anita Diamant Berke, Jim Rietmulder, and Ken and Carol Giniger for their patience and fortitude.

Prologue

THIS IS A DO-IT-YOURSELF BOOK. Anybody can use it, but it is written especially for those people who expect to celebrate America's 200th birthday party, the Bicentennial of the United States of America.

On July 4, 1776 the "Representatives of the *United States of America* in Congress assembled solemnly publish(ed) and declare(d) that these united colonies are FREE AND INDEPENDENT STATES." This was our Declaration of Independence. And it was the first time that the words "United States of America" were used. The time has come for us to celebrate "Brother Jonathan's 200th Birthday."

Of course, our nation was not created in a single day. The colonists had been talking and arguing about independence long before they adopted the actual Declaration, and they had done more than talk. Blood had already been shed—in Boston, at Lexington and Concord, at Bunker Hill, and in the backcountry. Just proclaiming the existence of a United States didn't change things overnight. An exhausting war had to be fought and a whole new form of government worked out. It took eight long years for the infant nation to become a reality.

At this writing, the Bicentennial Council of the Thirteen Original States suggests 1974-1989 as the period to be commemorated (from the first beginnings of provincial government through ratification of the Constitution). During this time Philadelphia, Boston (obviously connected with the events of the Revolution), Washington, and other centers typifying the growth of our nation, are talking about creating superduper spectacles.

But the spirit of the Bicentennial isn't sectional. The Commission confidently expects that "the Bicentennial will be national in scope. It has an appeal that will make every American eager to participate." They're right. Americans are individualists. They like to put on their own shows. From coast to coast people everywhere are studying and reading and preparing to dramatize their own commemoration of the Bicentennial.

This book is addressed to those people—to teachers in the elementary and high schools, to leaders in churches and church groups, to all sorts of youth organizations, to civic and patriotic societies, and to whole communities. The methods described in the following pages have been successfully tested in actual celebrations, large and small. Some were just class projects with only a few dollars to spend. Some were large projects with sizable budgets. The methods worked for both.

This is a practical book, based on experience.

For more than 35 years, the author has produced, directed, and/or written for such celebrations. Some of them, like the 175th Anniversary of the Declaration of Independence, the Railroad Show in Chicago, the Anniversary of the Battle of Gettysburg and Lincoln's Gettysburg Address, have been gigantic spectacles with generous budgets and coast-to-coast publicity. But more of them—like the Friends' Bicentennial in Sandy Springs, Maryland; the Hunter College 50th Anniversary in New York, and those of the Calvert School in Baltimore and the Syrian Junior League in Brooklyn—have been modest productions with limited funds, presented to a limited audience. One of the most successful was for the Jewish Tercentenary in Trenton, where there was almost no ready money in the till and where practically everything that went into the show was donated.

Over the years I developed an almost foolproof system of operations. In this book I describe that system. Everything that I talk about has been put to use, not once or twice, but many times. Some of the details are not very exciting reading, but they are necessary. Don't skip the parts describing these details. They may seem dry-as-dust, but they are absolutely essential to success. As in everything worthwhile, patience, dogged perseverance, creative enterprise, good planning, and periods of frustration are all parts of such an undertaking. But the result is worth the effort. The satisfaction that comes from the successful carrying out of such an enterprise is deep and lasting.

People who have taken part in a community or organizational or school spectacle always remember it. Every person who has ever had a theatrical experience gets a kick out of it, whether he works as a writer, an actor, a designer, or a less glamorous wardrobe assistant. There is nothing like the theater to bring people together and let them express themselves. There's a little bit of ham in everybody.

But there's more to putting on a celebration than personal satisfaction. The occasion serves as a showcase for hitherto unsuspected talents. It adds something to all participants' knowledge of history, to an understanding of the cooperation that goes into the creation of a work of art, and engenders a feeling of belonging to something. People of various ages, social habits, and ethnic backgrounds learn to work together. It solidifies the respect of participating groups for one another. It's a unique experience.

Never has there been an occasion that offers such unlimited scope for creative skill as the 200th anniversary of the birth of the United States. The President has appointed a commission to set up a great national celebration, but the anniversary has so many aspects that people from coast to coast will want to hold their own more modest celebrations in their own communities, in schools, churches, and patriotic societies. The signing of the Declaration and the war are only a part of the Revolution of 1776. The adoption of the Declaration of Independence was the visible symbol of a whole new era. The events of 200 years ago encompassed new ideas of liberty, of freedom, of the rights of man, of national aspiration, of the rule of law, of the separation of military and civil powers. Never before had a body of men deliberately set out to establish a nation of which the republican-democratic ideals were to be a foundation.

For 200 years Americans have been demonstrating their pride in their national aspiration. There are records of Fourth of July happenings, of celebrations of "Brother Jonathan's Birthday," even during the Revolutionary War itself. Descriptions are extant of elaborate dramatizations as far back as 1792. After the war, visiting Europeans were astonished by these celebrations and wrote lengthy accounts of them. Though they were often critical of the "obstreperous" American behavior and commented disparagingly on the amount of noise and the garishness that marked these occasions, they all, nevertheless, were impressed by the earnest spirit of patriotism underlying even the most outrageous displays. Everyone commented with respect on the obvious pride of the celebrants that their country, their own United States, was setting forth its ideals— freedom, liberty, and the rights of man. This pride was dominant no matter what the form of the occasion, whether a parade, fireworks display, a pageant or a re-enactment, or even a vulgar political wing-ding.

On our 200th anniversary we can do nothing better than to follow the example set by our fathers and grandfathers in dramatizing the struggle to attain and perpetuate these ideals.

Anniversary dramatic celebrations may take different forms, but whatever they are called, the problems of staging them are essentially the same. The only way to meet these problems is by setting up a strong, well-structured organization made up of executives, idea people, money raisers, technical specialists (director, designer, musicians, and multimedia people), and publicists. Call them chairmen or committees or councils or whatever you choose, they are the backbone of a successful celebration.

I have discovered that almost always the first question asked by people contemplating a dramatic presentation for anniversaries is, "Where do we find a script?" In the professional theater, where the play's the thing, this is of course the first concern. For the play is the basis on which the money is raised and the producer's organization set up. But in an anniversary celebration it is best to get going in just the opposite way: The money and help come in because of an idea, and the script must be tailored to fit the resources available. Before an actual dramatic script can be decided upon, the matter of organizing must be settled and a workable budget plan set up for carrying out the project.

Therefore, in this book I discuss the matter of organization before taking up the matter of script because, though celebrations may be simple or elaborate, large or small, inexpensive or astronomically costly, whether they are called parades or festivals or happenings or spectaculars, they are all basically pageants, and the manner of putting them on is fundamentally the same.

Because of this, I urge all prospective pageanteers to study the organizational chart at the end of Part IV carefully, and follow it as closely as possible even for the most modest productions.

This book is based largely on a series of lectures I gave at the American Theatre Wing Professional School of the Drama. The sequence here is the same as in my lectures. First comes Organization (Front of the House). Then comes Script. Then Organization (Backstage). Next, I lay down guidelines for creating, directing, and rehearsing the actual show, worked out after many years of experience. As an afterword, I treat briefly other related forms suitable for anniversary celebrations. And finally, there is a section entitled "Sources and Resources."

Most of the students in my class were totally inexperienced in the field of community dramatics, industrial shows, or in English and drama departments in schools and colleges, and none of them had ever worked with amateurs. They reported that what they learned from the lectures was a good foundation and most helpful when they were afterwards engaged in the actual work.

I hope my readers will find this book equally practical.

1 The Appeal
of the Pageant

EXPERIENCE HAS SHOWN THAT, of all the forms of drama, the pageant lends itself most effectively to the commemoration of historical events. So this book, although it will deal with all the usual commemorative methods, will concentrate primarily on the pageant. Hence, it should be of value to consider at the outset just what a pageant is, and what are its advantages and requirements.

A BRIEF HISTORY

A pageant is one of the oldest, simplest, and most exciting ways visually to dramatize a message. The ancient Greeks, as we know from friezes, used pageants, in addition to their great plays, to celebrate their religious festivals. In medieval times, religious tableaux presented on church holidays within the church building soon grew to be little plays enacted on the church or cathedral steps, telling some biblical story. Later, as the number of these plays increased, carts (called pageants) carrying the actors of each play would drive through the town, stopping at designated "stations" to perform. One of the earliest pageants of this sort that has come down to us is *The Story of Noah's Ark*.

In addition to the central plays, interludes would be included involving comedians, acrobats, jugglers, dancers, and musicians.

Little by little the acts lost their sacred character. They were driven from the church, but the pageant had become a regular feature of medieval life and developed as a secular art form in spite of growing church disapproval. *Everyman* is essentially a pageant; the chronicle plays of Shakespeare are truly pageants.*

Technically, the pageant is built on a single theme. It develops this theme through music, pantomime, words, color, dance, rhythm—what we call today multimedia—and above all, action. These combine to produce an emotional impact, an internal drama, doing away with the necessity for a formal plot.

THE TECHNIQUE OF THE PAGEANT

The pageant first of all must be visual. It must be something to be *looked at,* something in which design, movement, and color explain themselves and tell the story. In a way, a pageant can be compared with the old-time silent movie. Any sound serves merely to highlight and enhance that which is seen.

Change and contrast take the place of plot. A mass scene, for instance, may follow a "small" scene; a slow-moving scene, a busy one; a single voice, a chorus. There must be constant variety of color, of costume, of props. There must be variety in the selection of incident: a fight must be followed by a tender scene; a parade across the stage, by a scene between a few people. There must be variety in method: living people alternating or mixed with multimedia (movies, stills, enlarged photographs, perhaps even slogans on a screen); dancers coming after a static group. A stage play is more or less like an easel painting. In its visual composition, a pageant can be thought of as a mural. Each viewer should be able to see something interesting from any angle and should get the impression that the action continues after the actors leave the limits of the stage. In order to heighten this constant sense of change, there must also be a variety of accompanying voices, as in a Greek chorus. Since the kind of pageant of which we are speaking is likely to be done by amateurs, it is best to keep dialogue to a minimum and use narrators. But except for this, there is no limit to the variety of sound that can be used.

---

*See article, "Pageantry," by Adele Gutman Nathan, Blevins Davis, *Encyclopedia Americana,* Vol. 21, page 97, 1954 edition.

THE ADVANTAGES OF THE PAGEANT

A pageant is the most flexible of all dramatic forms. It can combine abstraction with reality, fact with fantasy. It can be enacted by professionals, or by amateurs, or by a combination of both. It can be performed by a few dozen people, or by hundreds. It can be big or little. It can be presented indoors or out; on a sophisticated stage or a simple platform; for limited audiences or thousands of spectators. Its scope and its form depend entirely upon the resources at hand, resources both human and monetary.

THE DEMANDS OF THE PAGEANT

Ideally, a pageant should run continuously with no intermissions. Scenes should flow from one to another, joined by bridges of action, narration, music, dances, or marches. There should be no blackouts, and certainly no theatrical curtain. Scenery should be kept to a minimum, and any scenery should be set in full view of the audience as part of the action. And even the most elaborate show should not run more than ninety minutes; indeed, less length is preferable.

There is no use planning a presentation comparable, let us say, with *Oklahoma!* on a budget of a hundred dollars, and without a star performer to take the lead "for free."

And yet, since even the smallest community is used to seeing well-produced motion pictures, there is no place for fakery. Big or little, expensive or modest, the effectiveness of any production depends on the strict maintenance of a standard of excellence within the scope of the possible. Sincerity, hard work, and good planning must take the place of professional competence. With no exception, the success of a dramatic celebration depends first of all on how thoroughly it has been planned in advance by the people in charge, how intelligently they understand their goal, and how skillfully they manipulate their resources. And, of course, it must be well rehearsed, primarily visual, and always fast-moving.

Part I

ooooooooooooooooooooooooooooooooooooooo

THE FIRST STEPS—
ORGANIZATION

2 How to Start
The Ball Rolling

LIKE EVERYTHING ELSE, pageant production must have a beginning. Let's consider how we can assure ourselves of the good start that is essential to a successful production.

MAKING THE DECISION

Many successful musicals begin with a few people and an idea. "Let's do a musical western style," somebody suggests, and the end result is *Oklahoma!* Many TV shows are developed in this way. The idea is first discussed by a few people with talent of one kind or another—talent for directing, talent for producing, talent for promoting, and, above all, talent for raising money.

An anniversary pageant may start the same way. Several people get together and propose that their community, school, lodge, or club join the national festivities for the Bicentennial of the American Revolution, and the result is a pageant.

Many matters must be looked into, however, before a hard decision can be made. Is our group or any other group interested? Have we enough time to do a decent job? Where will we get the money and how much? Is there executive talent available? Can we find appropriate performers and backstage help? Is there a convenient place to hold the pageant? And finally, how shall we get a script suitable to our particular locale?

How do we go about getting the answers to these questions?

THE STEERING COMMITTEE

Obviously, we need to be organized. And the first step toward organization is a steering committee. If you are going to get any pleasure out of *preparing* for the pageant (and that's half the fun), the steering committee should begin work as quickly as possible. For a community pageant two years in advance of performance isn't too much, and for a group pageant, twelve months is the minimum.

Naturally, the steering committee will include the two or three people who had the original idea. But can they put the idea over, without any help? The first thing needed is a good executive chairman.

EXECUTIVE CHAIRMAN

The executive chairman of the steering committee should also act as executive chairman for the entire project. He may not have had any theatrical experience, but he must have an intelligent interest in things cultural and he must be thoroughly sold on the whole idea. He must have a wide circle of friends, on whom he can call for money or help. He must be a person respected by the other members of the group or community who will back the enterprise, and he must be *absolutely nonpartisan*. He must have an understanding of financial matters, for although he will not deal directly with disbursements and contracts, he will have to oversee the person who does the work. And if he has a little charisma, it won't hurt.

A good executive chairman for a community-wide celebration would be a bank president, a department store owner or, perhaps, the mayor, if he is popular. A good executive chairman in a school might be the president of the student organization, a well-liked teacher, or a superintendent. Even a member of the board of education might fill the bill.

It is important that the executive chairman is used to being an arbitrator (there are constant uncertainties that pop up in any theatrical enterprise), and patient and able to deal with the temperament of persons involved. And he is the court of last resort for disputes between the director, the treasurer, the actors, and the authors. It always happens that people involved in dramatics get dramatic themselves. A good executive chairman, who knows how to keep his mouth shut, can generally help smooth over these rough places.

If, however, he cannot, and the whole project is threatened because of some silly dispute, it is the unpleasant job of the executive chairman to get rid of the dissenter, no matter who he is, if that is the only way to save the day.

The author remembers one executive chairman with especial tenderness. We were doing a pageant sponsored by a service group in a very small town in the deep South. We integrated the actors in the episodes without incident, but the costume chairman wanted her committee to function in segregated groups. This would certainly have resulted in bad feeling, but above all it was impractical. Almost all the really expert seamstresses available were black. How could they be limited to making costumes for black actors only! The executive chairman, who was a socially prominent woman and a leader in the community, solved the whole problem by inviting the entire committee, black and white, to an organizing meeting in her own home. Everybody came. She announced that she had arranged for the costume committee to work in the recreation rooms of a fashionable church. No further question of segregation was raised. The sound and fury simply evaporated.

In another case, the promotion and finance chairmen (whose function we describe later on), overanxious to get backing from business, promised the local radio station that the equipment they were going to lend would be marked prominently with the call letters of the station. They forgot that one of the real difficulties in using amplification in a pageant is to make the equipment as invisible as possible. The director asked the executive chairman to veto this promise. The executive chairman understood the situation and he succeeded in convincing the managers of the radio station that such blatant advertising was not to their advantage and that credit on the program would insure recognition.

Touchy problems of this sort are almost bound to come up. One of the less enjoyable tasks of the executive chairman is to get rid of people who turn out to be expendable. He may decide that the best way to do it is to kick them upstairs.

It's easy to see that the executive chairman is a V.I.P. He must be selected with care.

OTHER MEMBERS OF THE STEERING COMMITTEE

Among the initiators of the project there is probably one person who is hipped on local history. If not, a history fan will have to be recruited for the steering committee. Later on he will become the chairman of the historical research committee, but in the beginning his job is to gather material of a general sort which will help the steering committee to select a central theme for the celebration.

It's a good idea also to have someone on this committee who understands publicity. As soon as a pageant director is chosen, he too should sit on the steering committee. And if there are one or two people in the community or group who have no specific axes to grind and whose general advice and prestige would be useful, they may also be added.

But keep your steering committee small. Big committees make for argumentation.

It has been said that the ideal committee is a committee of three, two of whom never come to meetings!

THE THEME

In order to sell the project, the steering committee will have to settle upon a theme for the celebration. The theme sets the tone of the entire occasion. It must not be too specific; it must be a general concept.

The theme may be symbolic: Man's Opportunities and Responsibilities under Freedom; We Hold These Truths; For Patriot Dream; The Voice of Liberty; The Time is Now. Or idealistic: Freedom. Or realistic: Heritage; Homecoming. It may embody some special contribution that has been made locally to American history. The two hundred years of America are so varied that these can emphasize almost anything: the growth of religious freedom, broadening of educational opportunities, the fight for democracy, or the preservation of the environment. (There may be some local landmark around which you can build this topic.) Choose a slogan for the theme, one that will be in line with local aspirations, and is in the contemporary mood. For idealism, these days, must be couched in relevant terms, depending on world events. Because of this difficulty, the steering committee may prefer to use a realistic theme —"Brother Jonathan's Birthday" (a chronicle of America's past celebrations with a peek at the future), "Freedom for All" (the signing of the Declaration and its application to events of American history up to modern times), "From the Little Red Schoolhouse" (with examples of the events that have made possible ever broader opportunities for education). The list is almost endless.

OTHER DUTIES OF THE STEERING COMMITTEE

In the meantime the committee will be enlisting personnel for the front of the house committee and will look around for the specialists or professionals. As we have said, the steering committee must be organized as early as possible and well in advance of the proposed celebration, for the members must have plenty of opportunity also to explore the resources open to them. In this way they will be able to judge approximately how much money they will need for the project, where they will get it and in what form, and prepare a tentative budget.

TENTATIVE BUDGET

At this point in the proceedings it is not possible to make a firm budget. The best that the steering committee can do is to get enough money to set up an office and make a serious study, as they enlarge their organization, of the amount of money, donations of material, and volunteer help they can really count on. But before long they will have to establish an overall budget. This will be the determining factor in deciding the exact size and scope of their pageant.

However, for guidance, the items which *must* be accounted for in almost any celebration are set down on page 28. Some of them may be donated in kind, as for instance, office space; or the space for rehearsals and performances may be free except for janitor and clean-up service.

The allocations of money in the budget should not be rigid. In consultation the director and the steering committee chairman may decide to steal from one item to pay another as time goes on. But the overall budget should be scrupulously adhered to. However, in computing the budget, be sure to allow 25 to 30 percent over the computed total for unforeseen contingencies and price inflation.

BUDGET BREAKDOWN

Front of the House

(Approximately One Third)

Office Space (perhaps donated?)

Telephone

Secretary (perhaps volunteer?)

Stationary

Office Supplies (stamps, etc.)

Publicity (photos, posters)

Mailing

Advertising

Invitations, Tickets & Programs

Identification Cards

Typing of Lists & Instructions

Entertainment of Distinguished
Guests

Script Preparation (paper,
typing, etc.)

Bleachers, Scaffolding, Chairs
(if necessary)

Decorations (flags, etc.)

And most important of all,
Insurance

Backstage

(Approximately Two Thirds)

Costumes - Homemade
(materials, findings, place
for working)

Costumes - Rentals

Wigs & Makeup

Materials for Props & Scenery

Repair of borrowed historical
items

Music (copying)

Gratuities - Boy Scouts,
custodians, etc.

Transportation & Refreshments
for Volunteers

Trucking

Sound & Light Personnel &
Equipment

Entertainment of Distinguished
Participants

Rental of Multimedia

Rental of Hall, Theatre,
Stadium or whatever

Office (supplies, rental, etc.)

Telephone

Professional Help (Director?
Producer? Designer? Music
Director?)

*   *   *   *   *   *

And don't forget to allow 25% above budgeted items for unforeseen emergencies. And you must have a modest revolving petty cash fund.

3 Front of
The House

WHILE THE FUNCTION of the steering committee has mainly to do with policy, the members of the front of the house committee all must be workers in specific areas. They will be chairmen of subcommittees whose members in turn may have a particular job to carry on in the preparation or backstage doings of actual production.

FINANCE CHAIRMAN

The finance chairman, like the executive chairman of the steering committee, must be a leader in whatever group will underwrite the celebration. His first duty is to help the chairman of the steering committee in finding people to back the project. In addition, he must invent different sources of revenue. He must understand the overall budget and help set it up. One source of revenue which the finance chairman must explore is the possibility of charging for tickets. I myself prefer to charge for tickets rather than to give them away. An audience that lays out cash, no matter how small the amount, tends to appreciate the performance more than an invited audience. Paying clients are also more likely to show up on the night of the performance. Things people get for nothing are apt to be thought of as worth nothing. If tickets *are* to be sold, the finance chairman will arrange the setup, appoint assistants, and supervise the entire operation.

He should be a person with a broad outlook on financial matters rather than one who is preoccupied with bookkeeping details. He should appoint front of the house and back of the house treasurers, responsible to him, to handle day-by-day disbursement of funds. These people need not understand the fine points of production. Bank tellers, for instance, if properly supervised by a finance chairman with broad interests, make good treasurers. The author remembers one case in which a treasurer questioned a bill for "gelatin." "Must we feed the actors?" he asked. The finance chairman soon set him right by explaining that "gelatin" was the theatrical term for the color screens used in lighting.

It is the finance chairman who finally, in consultation with the steering committee chairman and the director, sets up the budget.

However, the question of how much actual cash must be raised by the steering committee will be determined as a result of the findings of the executive chairman of the steering committee, the finance chairman, and the community cooperation chairman, since the final cost of the celebration must be computed not only in cash but in the kind of volunteer services available.

CHAIRMAN OF COMMUNITY COOPERATION

The selection of the chairman of community cooperation is extremely important, for his activities and findings influence the work of several other committees. As we have already pointed out, many of his activities will have an effect on the work of the finance chairman, for it is he or she who will ferret out and bring the answers to many questions that will influence the making of the budget, and the kind of pageant to be planned.

The first of these questions has to do with a *place* suitable for the presentation of the pageant. Is there a playground, a school gymnasium, a church auditorium, a sports stadium, or perhaps even a theater that might be available? Because of the flexible nature of a pageant, any one of them might be suitable. But the question is: Can we get the site, not only for the performance, but for at least two rehearsals beforehand? Can we get the use of such a place free, or perhaps just for the cost of light, heat, and janitor service? Or must we pay a rental charge? The answer will influence the budget we must raise and, in turn, influence the kind of pageant we will put on.

Then there is the question of human resources. Are there any Little Theaters in town? Do they have dramatic directors, designers, or technicians (people who know about lights, sound, and so forth)? And, of course, actors? What kind of experience have all these people had?

The community cooperation chairman will tap other sources for recruits—the art schools and art departments in the high schools and colleges. Have they an imaginative leader who is knowledgeable about theatrical design? The chairman should also collect information about the school bands, the industrial musical ensembles and choruses in the vicinity, and find out whether they do rock or country music, patriotic and marching tunes, or are they "long-hair"? Is there a local chapter of the Musicians' Union in the vicinity who will help, perhaps, with money from the Musicians' Union Benevolent Fund. If there is a union local, will they allow us to mix recorded music with live musicians? And professionals in the pit with nonprofessionals in the cast?

In many communities a great deal of actual cash can be saved by getting help from the utility companies and the local radio or TV station. There are men and equipment in these places that can be useful, and perhaps can be "borrowed" without cost. The city government, the po-

lice, and the fire department can all help. And don't overlook the ubiq-
uitous Boy and Girl Scouts. Perhaps you may have to give a contribution to some organization like the PAL or the fireman's band, but that's
cheaper than having to pay outright.

The community chairman is in a position to suggest sources of supply
to other committee chairmen, and from the knowledge he has gained
he may have picked up some bits of local color that the chairman of
historical research may find helpful. But to repeat, his main job in the
early stages of organizing is to get to know about special groups, civic
organizations, unions, and city authorities who may be useful; to explore
the possibilities of appropriate sites, and to determine the response from
business houses and City Hall. Before long, he can probably make a
good estimate of how large an audience can be counted on and how
much popular enthusiasm there will be for the celebration. His report
will help determine, in addition to the amount of actual money that must
be collected, how many times and where and when it is practical to perform the pageant.

PUBLICITY CHAIRMAN

The publicity chairman is an important figure, not only in the early
stages of preparation but right straight through to the last "curtain." He
may already be one of the original members of the steering committee.
In theatrical parlance, the publicity man is responsible for bringing in
the audience for the show. In our pageant he must not only do this but
he must help "sell" the occasion to potential backers, like the utilities
companies (see Chairman of Community Cooperation) and people
who have usable technical resources. He must be ready to brief members of the steering committee and all other committees on the practical,
educational, and cultural benefits inherent in the scheme. He must explore the possibilities of getting publicity from the radio, TV station, and
the newspapers, and stand ready to supply them with interesting chit-
chat for columns and spot items which will keep the day-to-day interest
of the potential audience and of the participants too. The more names
he can mention the better, for it is the mothers and fathers and sons and
daughters of participants who will swell the audience.

All printing is the responsibility of the publicity chairman: posters,
invitations, handouts, car stickers, and the like. He may think it wise to
sell advertising space in the official program or he may even propose
charging for the program itself. These practices are not the best, in my
opinion, but a great many communities have adopted them. And the publicity chairman should have a good deal to say about whether or not to
charge for tickets. He may ferret out some way to make the tickets tax-

deductible by tying the occasion up with some local improvement. And if he is a good publicity man he will insist on plenty of very cheap seats or seats sold in blocks, for the important thing for good public relations is to have as cosmopolitan and as large an audience as possible.

The publicity chairman, in selecting his committee, will want the help of a photographer, and he should also have one or two people who act as his assistants so that someone from the publicity staff is present at all meetings of all committees, and at all rehearsals when that time comes. For it is at these small gatherings that things happen that make news.

HISTORICAL RESEARCH CHAIRMAN

The chairman of the historical research committee, like the publicity chairman, will probably be recruited from the steering committee. But like the publicity chairman, he still remains a part of the original group. He is simply adding to his duties.

What he has to do now is to create a committee which will go to work at once collecting historical data which will later on be used in connection with the script, with costume design, and perhaps even with music.

His best bet for members of his committee should be librarians, teachers of history and social sciences and, if there happens to be a historical society, the members thereof. There are probably also some local history fans and collectors of Americana whom he will find useful.

Too much emphasis cannot be put on the advantage of exploring the stories of events and the myths peculiar to the region. It is only the inclusion of local history that distinguishes one celebration from another, and stirs up community pride. Therefore the work of this committee should be to discover historic buildings that need restoration, and/or to suggest the placing of plaques and markers where historic landmarks, alas, no longer stand; statues and monuments ordinarily neglected can sometimes be made the center of the event. It's not too much to suggest that the historical chairman might even propose the planting of trees for peace, the dedication of a nature sanctuary, or the completion of a new school, all hitherto taken for granted, as the subject for a ceremony. Using such material which the historical committee has brought to the fore may well have a dramatic as well as an educational result and, in the end, cause participants and audience to see the relevance of history to modern times and their own daily lives.

Another job that the historical committee can do is to point out members of the community who may have made careers away from home. Such a favorite son or daughter might be induced to come back and take part in the celebration. At Winston-Salem in North Carolina, for example, Kathryn Grayson, the movie star, consented to take part in a scene in the pageant as a character at an antebellum ball. Dressed in a crinoline, she sang several songs of the period, accompanied by her then husband, the well-known song writer and producer, Johnny Green, who played on a small, mobile melodeon. Her return to her home town not only added to the quality of the pageant in which she participated but generated tremendous publicity and helped make it a great success.

In another pageant a local boy who had become an all-American football star in college appeared in a contest for a greased pig in a village market scene. He won, of course, to great applause and with much newspaper publicity.

Even in New York, not easily stirred by celebrities, this kind of thing is a useful gimmick. When Columbia University had its 200th anniversary, the producers of a commemorative pageant used Bennett Cerf, publisher and television personality and an alumnus, as narrator.

The historical committee, in almost any community, can come up with such a person.

Indeed there is no limit to the usefulness of such a committee if the members act with originality and resourcefulness. The possibilities are unlimited, for it will also be their job to marshal the facts that may be put to dramatic use in the script and be coordinated properly into the background of the celebration.

And in all cases of historical accuracy, the word of the chairman of historical research must be law.

IMPORTANT TO REMEMBER

Now we have broken down under individual committees the matters which must be taken care of that have nothing to do with the actual production of the pageant but which have almost everything to do with making the venture a success in the community. If it is a small event, perhaps one person can undertake two chairmanships. But this is a firm list of the business of the front of the house committee. Each item must be definitely assigned to a person responsible for carrying it out. This is the secret of every successful project; there must be no uncertainty about who is responsible for what.

The findings of this group are important to the eventual creation of the budget. One-third of that budget will be assigned to this group. We will find later on that some of the money that is allocated to them will be used to meet some of the costs of the backstage operation, as for instance, some of the printing bills for identification cards, etc. It may even prove to be economical to buy certain things that are necessary both front and backstage in one lump instead of piecemeal. If the front of the house committee objects to helping out that way, this group like everybody else must bow to the decision of the chairman of the steering committee.

Members of the front of the house committee should go into action as early as possible. Several of them may begin parts of their work almost simultaneously with the steering committee, as, for instance, the finance chairman, the historical research chairman, etc., but in no case should they incur expenses without the consent of the chairman of the steering committee. He alone will have a complete picture of the entire operation. The important thing is the pageant itself. There's no sense in spending money to build up public expectation unless the production is first class.

Part II

ooooooooooooooooooooooooooooooooooooo

THE KEY PEOPLE
OF THE PRODUCTION

4 The Backstage Specialists

THERE ARE CERTAIN ANGLES of the production which must be entrusted to people with some experience and special knowledge. These are the direction, the selection and perhaps even the writing of the script, the designing of the costumes, what scenery you may need, and the music.

THE DIRECTOR

The most important of these specialists is the *director*, who will be responsible not only for telling the actors what to do, but for overseeing and approving the work of all others. Therefore it is important that the steering committee, as one of its first acts, shall look around for a competent director, pin him down, and let him help make all decisions.

The director is the keystone of the production, and as long as he remains director, has the final word on all backstage decisions. Every person involved in the production must be willing to accept this, for without such authority the director is worth nothing.

A good director sees the production as a whole, like a general who understands the relative importance of *all* the units. With this knowledge he must have a free hand to map his strategy. Like the conductor of an orchestra or the architect of a building, he and he alone has the entire picture in mind. Only he is able to estimate the importance of each element. This includes choosing his own assistants, making the final selection of the cast, changing the script, and juggling the backstage budget.

The director must be free to adjust the script to the budget and the budget to the script. His advice is important in choosing the site. In a word, he has the responsibility of running all backstage affairs. And, to repeat, this authority must be well understood by everybody. Otherwise, he cannot put all of the details of the production together and blend them into a smooth continuity. He must have the confidence and backing of the executive chairman. Without this the production will become a shambles, and in that case the best thing to do is to fire the director and get a new one.

He must have technical know-how, tact, patience, and understanding of all the component parts—the budget, the script, the artistic design, the mechanical and technical workings, the music, the number and manner of rehearsals and how they are conducted. Beyond everything else, the director must have the ability to deal with the divergent personalities with whom he will certainly come in contact. This goes for the director of every show, no matter what its form, no matter how big it is or how small. No group is without its "know-it-alls" and dissenters.

Perhaps in the community itself such a person can be found. He may be the head of the dramatic department of the school or college. He could be a worker from the Little Theater group, or, in the case of a club, school, or church, someone who has already been successful in running other functions for that particular organization, and has the confidence of his fellows. Or perhaps there is someone in the local TV or radio station who can fill the bill.

However, there are advantages in getting a professional director from the outside. If at all possible, it is wise to spend what may seem at first glance a disproportionate percentage of the total budget on this one person. A good director is a good investment, and a money saver in the long run. He knows how to cut corners. He knows how and where to get things that seem ungettable. He can advise how costumes can be concocted from materials at hand, how a clever imitation can take the place of a rare original. Like an independent political figure, he has no previous commitments. He is willing to take the risk of becoming unpopular by deleting grandiose schemes that are beyond the reach of the project. He knows how to steal from one part of the budget to make up for a lack in another. All these skills make for economy, at the same time without losing quality. He will be unrelenting in his search for excellence, and will have a sophisticated standard of judgment.

There is another plus in having a professional. For some reason or other, a person who is being paid for doing a job, is in a more powerful position than a volunteer. Although he will be firm, he won't ride roughshod over the volunteers with whom he is working; yet his opinions will be taken more seriously by these same people. And since the success of any dramatic production depends on the participants' acceptance of the director's authority, anything that enhances this authority makes for a smooth-running show. Also, a professional knows he has a job to do, and if his work is not productive, he can be fired. But, amateur or professional, he is the kingpin of the production as long as he is director.

The kind of person you are looking for, if you decide to get a professional, is not a big-name Broadway-Hollywood type, but preferably someone who has been associated with community theater or so-called industrial shows. A person of this sort is used to handling amateurs and meeting a budget. His experience has made him down-to-earth and yet in touch with new ideas and new techniques. And his reputation will rest on bringing in a good production rather than on personal publicity.

Once a great show personality consented to come as consultant for a few days to a midwestern town. He arrived in his private plane (at the town's expense) with a secretary and two assistants, and spent most of his time in a leading hotel entertaining the newspaper people. He departed at the end of three days, leaving the pageant producers with no suggestions, all the detail work to do, and a big hotel bill, sizable bar bill, and transportation to pay.

Finally, if you do decide to engage a professional, it is important to have a written agreement. This will protect both you and the director.

In the early stages of organization, the director will need occasional—but regular—conferences, meeting with the steering committee and front of the house people. But at least ten weeks before production, all professionals must be on the ground constantly and always available. Many participants are amateurs with limited time to give—evenings, for instance, and odd lunch hours. On the other hand, the director and the staff must understand that *they are on duty seven days a week, twenty-four hours a day.* And when rehearsals begin, everybody will wish that the days were longer.

The names of some organizations who may be able to help find the kind of people you need to give professional assistance are listed at the end of this book in Part VIII under Sources and Resources—Professional Help.

THE DESIGNER

The designer is the chief assistant to the director in planning production. He should be a person with some technical training who understands the uses of color and line in establishing mood and creating variety. He must first make a comprehensive costume, prop, and makeup chart for the costume chairman and the casting chairman.

If the designer can make some little rough sketches, he can be a great help to the costume chairman in organizing and interesting people to work on the costume committee. He has studied period and knows how costumes ought to look when they're worn. He can design clothes which can be made easily or assembled by art classes, sewing circles, and even by mothers of actors.

Furthermore, the designer should be able to deal directly with costume rental houses and must understand contracts.

If there are character roles, he should provide authentic pictures to be copied by the makeup people. All makeup comes within his province.

He knows how scenery should be built and is able to instruct the people who do the actual building. He cannot be too temperamental for he must be able to work closely with a volunteer committee and to tactfully restrain the overmeticulous carpenters and detail-loving painters, explaining to them that scenery and props are, after all, temporary, most of them to be seen from only one side, not too carefully examined, and created exclusively for overall effect. This is especially true if the pageant is given at night and lights are used. This is mentioned here because it is one of the most difficult lessons to drive home to the carpenters, woodworkers, and do-it-yourself artists who are likely to make up the scenery and props committee.

The designer must also understand lighting and the place that lighting has in creating an effect. He must pass his knowledge on to the practical electricians who will make up the lighting committee. They are likely to know everything about electricity and nothing about the art of the theater, and are apt to resent what they call "impractical suggestions." Sometimes, however, these nontheatrical technicians can figure out cheap substitutes to get what the designer wants.

Before vehicles are used, he should see that they are in the correct period. Nothing is more foolish than a rubber-tired buggy representing a one-horse shay.

The designer's overall contribution is his understanding of the use of color, light, and contrast in the establishment of mood and the maintenance of correct period. In a more mundane field, he should keep an eye on small expenses—hardware, paints, lumber, and even needles, pins, and especially scissors.

A competent designer is an excellent bit of insurance against exceeding the budget.

THE MUSIC DIRECTOR

Of almost equal importance with the designer is the music director. Perhaps the historical research chairman has been able to dig up traditional music or perhaps the music director will have someone on his committee to assist him to do this special job. But the music director himself must be able to write an occasional "bridge" or create or assemble a background continuity—a music script against which the pageant moves. Ideally, he will also understand how to conduct a chorus, an orchestral group, or a band. If not, he will know where to find people who can do this under his supervision.

Details of the job of the music director and his committee will be discussed in the section Fitting the Music into the Script in Part III and in the section on music in Part VIII.

OTHER SPECIALISTS

Undoubtedly the specialists will want to select other assistants. The director will have to have a general stage manager, *his* assistants, a casting and recruiting committee, and a special events committee to carry on the executive portion of bringing in the show. The designer may divide his requirements among a costume committee, scenery and props committee, and an effects committee, and the music director may want people to help him in his work. The duties of these assistants will begin later and will be discussed in Part VI.

Now is the time, in consultation with the director and the other specialists, to re-examine the budget and bring it up to date. Next, without further delay, a definite script should be decided upon.

Part III

○○○

THE SCRIPT

5 When and Where
to Look for
Script and Writers

UP TO NOW we have been concerned with an idea, and the people who will handle the practical problems connected with it. The time has come to put that idea into the workable words we call the script.

NECESSITY FOR DELAY

It's high time, the reader may think, but our reasons for putting it off until now have been practical. Before we could really decide on a script, we had to know how many and what kind of people would be interested in acting or helping backstage. We had to know how much money we could figure on having. And how large or small or cheap or expensive our physical site would be. For on these realistic considerations the choice of our script must largely depend. We have come to the point where we have a pretty good working answer to these questions. So we can take up the fascinating matter of the script.

Not that this matter has been forgotten. The script has been bobbing up persistently in one way or another ever since the first moment when we started to think of a celebration. Those unquenchable enthusiasts—

the historical researcher, the idea man, and the director—have been doggedly ferreting out ideas about the script and tossing them into discussions all through the process of organizing, and especially when the subject of the general theme has come up. However, they did not get the attention, up to this point, that they thought they deserved.

But now the steering committee, the front of the house chairman, and the director have satisfied themselves about the money they probably can collect through contributions, whether they should or should not sell tickets, what kind of stunts they might put on to swell the exchequer, what free help is available, the dramatic and technical talent on tap; and they have located space for preparation and presentation. With this work done, the main attention of everybody is turned to the matter of the script.

THE READY-MADE SCRIPT

Perhaps the historical chairman and his committee, in their research, have come across an already written script that seems to be suitable. They have combed the catalogues of the publishers who specialize in historical presentations for amateurs, and they have found something which they like. Or perhaps they have read some book which they think could be transformed into a pageant. Or one act of a patriotic play that lends itself to such expansion. Or some local scrivener may have submitted a work that has met with their approval.

But it is pretty certain that any work that has been written without a thorough knowledge of the physical and material potentialities and the talent on hand must be adapted to local needs. It must be tailored to fit the peculiar capabilities and conditions of this one particular production. Of course, to do this, the permission of the original writer is necessary. But experience has shown that a ready-made script, like a dress bought off a rack, needs alterations, since every production, like the human figure, varies in detail.

Take the matter of dialogue, for instance. It's almost certain that very few of your amateur actors know how to put over spoken lines intelligibly. To teach them to do so, even if it were possible, entails long, hard work, and individual attention from the director. Therefore it is invariably wiser and more practical to transfer the speeches and dialogue to narrators.

Although in some pageants only one narrator is used, I admit a preference for several—two or three, or even four. These narrators should have voices easily distinguishable one from the other—a deep voice, a light voice, a youthful voice, and certainly, a woman's voice. In almost every community it is possible to find people in the radio station, in a lawyers' association, on a college faculty, or among persons accustomed to public speaking, who can function as narrators. In some cases, these people will not even be visible to the audience, and so they can read their lines. They should all be provided with microphones. Their prime function is to be understood by the audience.

So, in doctoring our basic script, practically all of the dialogue should, without question, be assigned to the narrators. In this way we can preserve the variety one gets from dialogue and do away with the mumbling so trying to the audience and destructive of effect.

Another example of how to doctor a ready-made script is to introduce local references, or perhaps even a whole episode having to do with local history. And don't forget the hometown boy who made good, mentioned earlier.

Still another variation on the script is the introduction of what might be called "professionals." At the 175th Anniversary of the Declaration of Independence at Independence Hall, Philadelphia, there were small scenes on an inner stage, showing groups of delegates from different states conferring—Thomas Jefferson, John Adams, and William Mason discussing the draft of the Declaration on which they have been working and Benjamin Franklin and Robert Morris persuading the Pennsylvania dissidents to change sides. All these parts were played by members of the Pennsylvania Bar Association. Between these small scenes, sometimes simultaneously, the other people in the cast, representing the Philadelphia citizens, moved back and forth on the large forestage, pursuing their daily activities. A market wagon stopped and a group of Philadelphia housewives bought vegetables. The Reverend Duché, pastor of Christ Church, and Rabbi Seixas entered with members of their congregations, and greeted each other. John Hancock arrived, surrounded by a party of singing Liberty Boys. In this way the variety necessary in a pageant was added to the basic story—that of the adoption of the Declaration. Atmospheric movement such as this can be injected into almost any ready-made script.

Don't hesitate to juggle or rewrite any part of the script that goes beyond your powers of presentation. Understand your own limitations. Each individual producing group is capable of only so much, and the script of any successful pageant must not make demands that can't be met by the participants. It's better to do something simple with style than something grandiose with no distinction.

One of the matters which may call for changes in a ready-made script is the selection of the setting in which our pageant is to be presented. Perhaps the place which we have of necessity chosen is a school auditorium with a shallow platform and a large front apron, or a newly built theater with what is called a "thrust stage." Or perhaps even a stadium or a playground in which we use nothing but an irregular platform. But the favored script has been written to be played on a more conventional stage with a proscenium. The director and his associates in such a case must not hesitate to make any changes in the script that are dictated by structural considerations. In a word, the director and his associates must be ready to make changes that are necessitated not only by the human and financial resources at hand, but by practical production problems as well.

In short, no prefabricated pageant will cover all the specialized circumstances of each and every community. It must be doctored.

Above all, the slogan should be "Be flexible." As the actual production begins to evolve, and especially during rehearsals, new possibilities will unfold, perhaps from the skillful creation of "extras" during rehearsals. But in all cases of change, it is the director who must have the last word, and changes must be limited to those which are within the overall pattern; preferably they must be historically accurate, and approved by the historian. But even the historian must be willing to allow for a bit of dramatic license.

All this is very trying for the author. It's no pleasure for him to stand by and see his precious manuscript manhandled. Yet every writer for the theater, unless he is also the "angel," must steel himself to this experience. The author remembers in her "salad days" being present at a rehearsal of *Mourning Becomes Electra* when Eugene O'Neill was asked to make changes. And he did. One shudders to think how Shakespeare would feel today witnessing some of the stunts and interpretations that have been injected into *Hamlet.*

Let me warn you again, however, that if you intend to make some changes, you must have absolute carte blanche from the author. Of the many pageant scripts on which the writer has worked, the most trying to produce was one with some literary merit, which had been written in advance by an established local author. As he envisaged it, we would have had to present it on stage with the automated technical equipment of the Metropolitan Opera House of Lincoln Center, New York, a budget the size of that for *My Fair Lady* and a roster of Broadway stars. The writer declared his whole-hearted cooperation and seemed to understand our problems. But every change in the script made necessary by lack of money or the limited ability of amateur actors or the fact that we were producing it in a stadium when he had written it for a theatre—each one of these was the occasion for a heart-breaking offstage scene. The author, like all authors, had a real pride in his brainchild. It was an extremely delicate matter. He told everyone about his troubles. As a writer he was well regarded, indeed even revered in his hometown, and the situation might easily have ended in a production-wrecking row involving all the actors. The steering committee chairman stood four-square behind the director, but even so, the continuing feeling engendered an atmosphere that threatened the pleasant relations of the early rehearsals and would have detracted from the enjoyment of the participants in the entire rehearsal period and even the project itself, if it had not been settled.

THE CUSTOM-MADE SCRIPT

On the other hand, one of the most successful, though modest, pageants ever directed by me was written by a committee. It won for itself and for all the staff involved, a Regional Valley Forge Freedoms Foundation Award.

By and large, my choice for a pageant script is one written to order, preferably by a group.

The very character of a pageant makes "writing-it-yourself" possible. Rarely is a pageant a piece of literature. The most important thing is the action scenario. It is something to look at, not something to listen to. The first requirement of a good pageant, as we have said before, is movement, variety, color, and sound effects, which include the words. It is this emphasis on eye appeal that makes it possible, and indeed sometimes preferable, for more than one person to write the script.

For instance, the words of the pageant that celebrated the 175th anniversary of the Declaration of Independence at Philadelphia were written by a newspaper man, after a scenario by the director and the historian. The vignettes at the 100th anniversary of the Battle of Gettysburg were written by a woman civic leader and were tailored to fit different landmarks selected in advance by the editor of the newspaper, a historical buff, and the director, in consultation with the writer.

The 300th anniversary pageant of the landing of the Society of Friends in America was written by the Board of Overseers of the Friends' Meeting.

Even the most distinguished writers have been willing to accept this procedure—scenario first, narration after. For instance, Catherine Drinker Bowen wrote the prologue for the 175th anniversary celebration of the Declaration. And in the re-enactment of *Mr. Lincoln Goes to Gettysburg,* the historic and imaginative narration was written by the distinguished playwright Marc Connelly, after a scenario by the director. The descriptive part of the script was added at the dress rehearsal with the help of the well-known commentator Ben Grauer. It turned out to be an ideal arrangement. The pageant won a National Freedoms Foundation Award, and copies are featured in the New York Public Library of the Performing Arts, the Brown University Lincoln Library in Providence, Rhode Island, and the Enoch Pratt Free Library in Baltimore.

HOW TO FIND WRITERS

In every community, club, or school, there are people who, for one reason or another, are used to putting words together. They may be teachers of English or history in a local school or college. They may be writers for the hometown newspaper. They may work in the TV or radio station, or they may be professors of the social sciences who use multimedia in their classes. Or club members who are in the habit of making reports and presenting papers. These people should be ferreted out by the chairman of community cooperation. Bring your group of potential writers together with your general chairman, historical research and idea man, and the director. Brief them on the practical side of the project: the budget, the technical limitations, the site selected for presentation, and the actors available.

Now they are ready to discuss the subject matter of the pageant script.

6 What Shall We Write About?

ANY DIFFICULTY PRESENTED by this question is usually not due to the lack of subject material but rather to the wealth of choices. Your choice must be made while keeping in mind appropriateness and audience appeal, your resources in personnel, money, and material, and where you plan to stage your show.

BATTLES

Almost certainly someone will come up with the subject of battles. There is so much action in a battle and so much color and fanfare that the re-enactment of a battle seems an obvious choice for a pageant. But here is a word of warning. Re-enactments of battles, to be at all realistic, require enormous casts. They are hard to plan, and even when well planned, are difficult to control. The truth is that though the participants have a roaring good time, battle re-enactments are almost always confusing and boring to the audience. To coin a phrase, when you've seen one cavalry charge, you've seen them all. So, even though the battle occurred near the scene of the pageant and cries out to be included in any local story, it is better to use the event itself as an incident or perhaps as the climax toward which to build a pageant than to do just a long battle re-enactment instead of a pageant.

Experiences of producers during the anniversary of the Civil War, even with the assistance of the trained Army and plenty of money to spend, resulted in complete disenchantment with re-enactments of battles. The Battle of Bull Run (or Manassas), which was the kickoff of the centennial years' commemorations, was a complete disaster, theatrically speaking, just as the original was in the real Civil War. But this was not the result hoped for. The re-enactment of the Battle of Antietam was long and wearisome, and the audience actually laughed when a regiment of Confederates rushed onto the field at a critical moment. The truth of it was that the audience didn't really know what was going on. The reenactment of Pickett's Charge at Gettysburg, which involved 3,000 Sons of Confederate Veterans and Sons of Union Veterans of the Civil War plus a company of well-trained soldiers from the Third Army, was an unimpressive mixup. Since your author herself was responsible for that, she may say that it was anything but a success.

Almost all of those involved in the staging of Civil War battles are ready to admit that these re-enactments, obviously full of pageantry and seemingly simple to stage, are the dramatic expression most difficult for amateurs to put on with any dignity. It takes a real professional to stay dead after he's shot down, and the sight of supposedly dead soldiers getting up and leaving the scene of action is, alas, laugh-provoking. In other words, it's best to keep combat action to a minimum. There are too many technical difficulties involved. Besides, it is important to remember that the battles were only part of the Revolution, although perhaps at first glance they are the most readily re-enacted, and in the light of our present-day ambivalence toward armed conflict, it is well to recall that a very important and dramatic aspect of the Revolution was the constant effort of the civilian leaders to prevent a takeover by the military— a principle still relevant.

MEMO   From: Mrs. Nathan, Director
        To: Mr. Davis, Writer

ROUGH SCRIPT OUTLINE - "INDEPENDENCE!"

Time

(1)   11:00 AM   Band Concert. *No* "*Star Spangled Banner!*"

(2)   11:30 AM   Dignitaries Enter.

(3)   11:35 AM   Greetings & Speeches. *Short!!*

(4)   11:55 AM   Entrance from Walnut St. thru audience,
                    Yankee Doodle, Narrator, with Fife &
                    Drum Corps - Prologue. *March - Fanfare*

(5)   12:05 PM   Narrators to Podium - Pageant begins.
                    (There are 2 Narrators - Yankee Doodle + Modern)
(6)   12:10 PM   Morning, July 4, 1776 - Tensions of
        Long Narration   Loyalists & Libertarians stressed,
                    gradual gathering, workmen, school
                    children, farmers, vendors, ladies &
                    gentlemen of Philadelphia. *Band on Stage?*

(7)   12:40 PM   Signers gather & enter Independence Hall.

(8)   12:46 PM   Street scene - waiting for news. Colonial
                    soldiers, Sons of Liberty, some Red Coats
                    added to scene. Reverend Douché & Rabbi
                    Seixas meet.

(9)   12:50 PM   Entrance, Caesar Rodney (mounted) thru
                    audience. He rushes into Independence
(9A)   Hall. Crowd tension. Small boy bursts
                    from door, rushes to front stage & looks
                    up to Bell Tower. Excitement mounts.

(10)   12:55 PM   "Ring, Grandfather, Ring!"

(11)   1:00 PM   Signers enter from Independence Hall.
                    Jefferson with document to Podium to
                    read. Bells, peal *(Bells! Bells! Bells!
                    Everywhere).*
(12)   1:10 PM   All exit led by Yankee Doodle, Fifes &
                    Drums, modern Color Guard - march thru
                    audience to Walnut, right on Walnut to
                    Sixth, around Sixth to Chestnut entrance
                    & disperse inside Independence Hall.

                                            AGN.

THE SIGNING OF THE DECLARATION—
REALISTIC TREATMENT

In addition to battle re-enactments, another obvious subject for a bi-centennial celebration is, of course, the actual signing of the Declaration of Independence. The event is well documented; it could be realistic and historically correct, and it certainly is noncontroversial.

But is such a re-enactment a pageant? The answer is: NO. There is no visual action. The contest is between ideas. There are no fist fights, duels, or any kind of personal encounters involved, that constitute action. The tension must be developed through dialogue. It would make a splendid television documentary; but though it seems to promise an interesting conventional play, except for the musical *1776* produced in New York in 1969, no play of this kind has yet been a success.

If the scene of the signing is to be used as a pageant, it must be "pageantized." What do I mean by "pageantizing"? Let me give you an example. Following is a detailed account of the Independence Day Pageant which was presented in Philadelphia on the 175th anniversary of the signing of the Declaration.

There was a problem—the site of the pageant. It was to take place in front of Independence Hall. The facade of the building itself was to be our backdrop, the paved space in front of it, our stage, with the audience sitting in the park facing the structure. Since it was a daytime performance, we could not use any other scenery. All we had were the fine broad steps leading up to the front door, and an arcade on each side, as wings. Once the signers went inside the building, anything they would do would be lost to the audience.

Faced with these limitations, we decided to do a pageant which would represent the day in Philadelphia on which the delegates were to meet to adopt or reject the document which had been prepared by Jefferson, Adams, and Morris; the arrival of the delegates; the behavior of the citizens during the time that the debate was going on inside; and the reception given the public announcement that the Declaration had been adopted.

We evolved a simple one-page scenario (see the reproduction), created by the director and the idea man. As you can see from following this scenario, we started the pageant with music and a procession. From the back of the park comes first a drum and fife corps playing "Yankee Doodle." Following are three characters unmistakably representing the famous painting *The Spirit of 1776* (a little corny but well within the comprehension of the most diverse audience). Last of all comes Yankee Doodle himself (in this case played by Maurice Evans, the well-known actor). Up the center aisle marches the procession. Yankee Doodle mounts the steps where there is hidden a microphone. His escort ranges around him. The music stops and Mr. Evans reads the Prologue, written to order by the distinguished historian, Catherine Drinker Bowen. It is a literary composition, not much more than a page long. When he finishes reading it, and to a musical accompaniment, he withdraws to the left side downstage, where there is a small platform on which Ronald Reagan and Robert Ryan, in ordinary clothes, have already taken their places. They are narrators, using a script written by Burton Davis, the theatrical critic of the *New York Tribune.* The actual pageant begins.

"Philadelphia, July 4, 1776. The day began like any other day . . ." Then the narrator goes on to outline the events that have preceded this day: the meeting of the Continental Congress, the introduction of the Virginia Resolves, the fact that today is the day on which, inside the building (and he describes the room), the delegates are to vote for the rejection or adoption of the Declaration of Independence.

While the narrators fill in the background, the citizens of Philadelphia begin to gather. First of all comes the watchman, calling "Six o'clock and all's well." One by one he extinguishes the lights in the square and around the building. Now tanners, shoemakers, wheelwrights, blacksmiths come in on their way to work. They gather in little knots. They are discussing the day's coming events. Some point to the windows of the room in which the meeting is to take place. Now children appear on their way to school. Then, as housewives, farmers with their wagons, and food vendors come and set up their stands, the signers come drifting in, sometimes singly and sometimes in groups. They pause and greet each other, but their whole demeanor is more purposeful than the rest of the crowd, and after stopping for a few minutes' talk, they mount the steps and go through the door into the building. As each prospective signer appears, a narrator identifies him. "There is John Dickinson from Pennsylvania. They say he is opposed to the Declaration." "Here in this group just appearing is Dr. Benjamin Franklin. He is the best-known member of the Congress. He looks tired. He has been working all night trying to persuade the other members of the Pennsylvania delegation to go along with him in approving the Declaration." And so on.

The narrators also point out several people in the crowd who are not signers. "There is Mistress Drinker, a Quaker lady hot for independency." "The Pastor of Christ Church, the Reverend Jacob Duché, who is coming into the Square to see what is happening. He joins Rabbi Seixas." The last of the signers to arrive is John Hancock. He drives up in a coach drawn by an exuberant crowd of his staunch supporters, the Liberty Boys. Descending from the coach, Hancock makes his way through the citizens of Philadelphia, greeting them with a political savvy. After a flamboyant adieu to his followers, he disappears into the building. The momentous meeting has begun. It takes place offstage out of sight of the audience.

Now we have to invent something to keep the audience interested while the signers are in session. Here is the place for an interlude, a busy market scene. Housewives are trading with vegetable hucksters. Vendors are selling pies, flowers, balloons. Friends are meeting and gossiping. A farmer with a cow is selling milk. Water carriers and fish mongers, trundling their barrows, cry their wares. Businessmen gather in anxious knots and stand on tiptoe to peep into the windows of the State House. Throughout the scene there is an air of expectancy. Tension mounts. While this is going on, the narrators have been describing the debate inside. "There is a deadlock," they say. At this moment there is a shout and a man on horseback comes riding through the audience. His face is muffled and when he dismounts he totters up the steps into the hall. "This is Caesar Rodney," the narrators say. "He is dying of an incurable disease but he has ridden all the way from Delaware so that he can take part in the debate. How will he vote? If he votes 'aye' and the Declaration is accepted, the bell in the tower, the bell inscribed 'PROCLAIM LIBERTY THROUGHOUT THE LAND' will ring forth the news."

Suddenly a small boy bursts through the great door. Turning his back to the audience, he points up to the bell tower. The crowd on stage turns to look where he is pointing. Narration stops. In the sudden silence the single childish voice is heard crying out, "Ring! Grandfather, ring!" (The boy has been rehearsed in the part, instructed to count nine slowly to himself and shout his line on the tenth count.)

Immediately the bell in the tower begins to peal. The center door opens wide, and Thomas Jefferson, holding up the document, comes out on the steps, followed by the signers. The narrator: "When in the course of Human Events, etc., etc." Bells hidden all around the square join one by one in the ringing. A tremendous cacophony fills the air. The narrator's voice fades. Jefferson, Franklin, Adams come slowly down the steps of Independence Hall. Followed by the entire cast, they march straight through the audience and out of sight. Last in the procession is Yankee Doodle; his fife and drum corps tooting triumphantly.

And here let us point out that the triumphal exit march of the cast is a "must," for it takes the place of a final curtain.

The episode of the boy, of course, is an example of dramatic license, for the story is a myth—dubious history, but good theater.

From this description the reader can see what we mean by "pageantizing" an event. There might be other ways of doing this. If this pageant had taken place at night we might have actually represented the debate by the use of spotlights. Or if the setting had been a different one, on a conventional stage, the signing might have taken place in an inner "box" and flashbacks, held together by processional or by musical interludes, might have taken place on the forestage. In this case there might have been a scene enacted around each signer, showing him back in his own bailiwick, receiving his instructions before he left for the Congress.

But in any case, no matter what the treatment, there would have been action scenes and a variety of sound, music, cheering and, of course, visual action.

This is what we mean by "pageantizing."

PAGEANTS BASED ON IDEAS

In the story of the founding of the United States, its growth and development, there are, in addition to actual incidents, ideals and aspirations that may well be pageantized.

Even a realistic treatment of the actual signing could be developed with attention to the ideas in it instead of to the events. The philosophy in the Declaration might be visualized. The rights of man. The growth of democracy. The establishment of a nation under law. Each of these concepts might be represented in a series of small scenes and mass movement which, with appropriate narration, sounds, and music, would make good theater. They might, for example, be written as a series of simple flashbacks combined with historical episodes which would dramatize the struggle for each principle, and its development to the present day.

What was it in the American experience that differentiates it from the revolutions that we know in our own time? What did these revolutionists have in their background that prepared them to set up a workable republican government?

A pageant on this subject might include such episodes as the scene of the Mayflower Compact, John Adams defending the British officers who took part in the Boston Massacre, Patrick Henry and the Virginia House of Burgesses, and Andrew Hamilton and Peter Zenger fighting for freedom of the press. What gorgeous processionals we could have—early fighters for free thought like Rousseau and Locke, Roger Williams, Ann Hutchinson, Governor Carver and John Winthrop, and even including Moses and the prophets, for it was from them that the New Englanders received their inspiration of a community living freely under law. Jefferson and Madison with the Founding Fathers, William Lloyd Garrison, Horace Greeley, Harriet Beecher Stowe, Lucy Stone, and Amelia Bloomer. Frederick Douglass and Martin Luther King. All "doing their

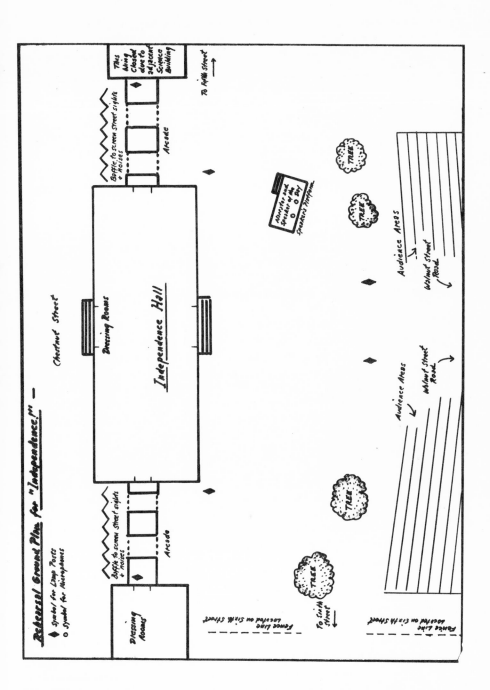

Rehearsal Ground Plan for "Independence."

♦ Symbol for Lamp Posts
○ Symbol for Microphones

Chestnut Street

Independence Hall

Dressing Rooms

Dressing Rooms

Arcade

Arcade

Baffle to screen Street sights + noises

Baffle to screen Street sights + noises

This Wing Closed due to adjacent Science Building

To Fifth Street

Amplifier and Speaker of the Day

Speakers' Platform

TREE

TREE

TREE

TREE

Audience Areas

Audience Areas

Walnut Street Road

Walnut Street Road

To Sixth Street

Fence Line Located on Sixth Street

Fence Line Located on Sixth Street

own thing" and all representing fighters for liberty and democracy.

Or if we choose to emphasize the growth of a national consciousness we could have scenes from the French and Indian Wars, when the Colonists began to think of themselves as Americans and to cooperate with each other in their own defense. Or Benjamin Franklin, proposing a joint Congress of the Colonies when the "Don't Tread on Me" flag was adopted. Or Sam Adams addressing a caucus in Faneuil Hall. We have Paul Revere as a representative of the Committees of Correspondence. Nor must we forget the continuing struggle for national consciousness. The Civil War. The muckrakers and the New Deal.

The possibilities are limitless.

REGIONAL SLANTS

Each locality has its own distinctive contribution to celebrate, not only in the Revolution but to modern America as well. Of course, the events in the East are known to practically everyone. Massachusetts has Lexington and Concord, the Boston Tea Party, Bunker Hill. But New England also had the first free schools, and Rhode Island the first Negro regiment. At Philadelphia the signers met in Independence Hall. And New Hampshire established the first college for Indians—Dartmouth. Pennsylvania, North Carolina, Kentucky, and Tennessee as well as Rhode Island gave asylum to religious refugees.

But on the other hand, Ohio, Illinois, Indiana, Michigan, Wisconsin, and Minnesota were opened up by George Rogers Clark, and it is here that the whole western syndrome, promulgated by Frederick Jackson Turner, began to make itself felt. Iowa was the first state to introduce woman suffrage. The states of the Western Reserve were the first to allocate portions of their territory by law to colleges.

Every section of the country has its own individual chapter in the American story.

Without regard to state boundaries, ethnic groups—Germans, Jews, Scandinavians, Italians, Negroes—have their own tales to tell in our overall struggle for freedom. And every one of these stories—and dozens more—lends itself to dramatic presentation, which gathers strength from its local application.

It's not difficult in any community to discover incidents like those mentioned. Undoubtedly our idea people have already tapped the local source of supply. They have no doubt already enlisted the help of the town librarian who for many years has had a special interest in the folklore of the region.

In most communities there is some historical society or club which has been happy to put its resources at the service of the researchers. And there must be some "oldest inhabitant" who is only too grateful to be allowed to recall the legends and myths that have been handed down through generations.

As we pointed out earlier, local landmarks are a fruitful source of ideas. The restoration of historic buildings or the placing of plaques and markers where historic buildings no longer stand, the planting of trees for peace, the dedication of a nature sanctuary, the completion of a new school—each of these can be pageantized. Or, in the light of the present preoccupation with the environment, a whole dramatic presentation might be devoted to the completion or the inauguration of some preservation project that could easily be tied in to the chosen Bicentennial theme.

PARADE PAGEANTS

Don't hesitate to move from place to place. A pageant can turn into a sort of parade involving the audience, with scenes taking place in different locations.

Actually, a very good conventional parade with a central theme could be constructed on the subject of the signing. The principal float, of course, would be the event itself. Other units could deal with subjects leading up to it and stemming from it; and plenty of color and sound and music would be appropriate where there would be groups of Revolutionary soldiers, British redcoats, Hessians, Liberty Boys, Boston Tea Party Indians, Minute Men, and so on. Place loudspeakers at selected spots so that a background of narration accompanies the parade. Conventional parades are described in Part VII.

SUGGESTED BACKGROUND MATERIAL

One of the most interesting and rewarding aspects having to do with an anniversary celebration is the impetus it gives to everyone connected with it to get acquainted with the new history of the background on which it is based. While chairman and actors are indulging themselves in this as a sort of recreation, it is a must for the director, the designer, the music director, and especially the people who have anything to do with the script.

Fortunately, a whole school of historians today are dedicating themselves to enlarging the scope of American history, to making it human and presenting it in a form that will be entertaining to the layman as well as to the scholar. While the emphasis in the old textbooks was on battles, dates, and political events, the new writers deal with what we call "social studies." They deal with the people, the customs of the day, the home life, the personal conflicts, the problems of the farmers, the merchants, the lawmakers, the churches, the women and children, and the minorities. Several of these new history books have been written so entertainingly that they have become best sellers.

This writing of new history was ushered in by Charles and Mary Beard, Vernon L. Parrington, Arthur Schlesinger, Sr., and their group. At first they were greeted by a storm of protest and called "muckrakers of American history." But their books are a great help to the dramatist, for they introduce us to lesser-known characters who make fine additions to a pageant cast. Furthermore, they are invaluable in helping us to choose themes for the Bicentennial, for they deal with such subjects as the development of a new kind of human experiment—the establishment of a republic, with the struggles of the Congress under the Articles of Confederation to preserve civil control over the military, and the conflict over the slave question, for example.

The titles and publishers of some of these books are listed in Part VIII, Sources and Resources, under Historical Background. Most of them are readily available at any high school or university library, and make exciting reading.

7 Anatomy of a Script

SCRIPT WRITING FOR A PAGEANT is a specialized form of dramatic writing. At this point it will be well for us to review the process.

DEVELOPING A SCRIPT

Presumably we have our writers, our subject, and our director. Next we evolve, out of our research, a simple scenario with dramatic possibilities. The job now is to build this scenario into a workable script.

In a stage play the stage directions are interspersed with the speeches, but a pageant script must be set up differently, for the action and the words take place at the same time; while the words must *cover* the action, they do not necessarily spring from it.

The writers of the words must always keep this in mind. Therefore, in writing a pageant script, the stage directions or action and the words and sounds must be set down parallel to each other. Here is a simple mechanical trick by which the writers of the words will always be reminded of this:

Take a piece of regular typewriter paper and turn it sidewise. Divide it into three columns: Column No. 1—Voice; Column No. 2—Action; Column No. 3—Sound and Music. In the second column the action is described. In the first column are the words to be spoken. In the last column, we indicate the background music, the incidental sound, and any sound effects (see the reproduction in this section of one page of the rehearsal script for the 175th anniversary celebration of the Declaration of Independence).

This is the method to follow, whether you use a ready-made or a custom-tailored pageant. Here you have your basic working script. By keeping the different parts of the pageant separate, they can be rehearsed separately.

As rehearsals go on, you may want to add another column for action detail. Or you might want to write down a list of the cast as it comes on the stage. When you have this playing script typed, leave a lot of space between the lines and between scenes *so that there is plenty of room for anything you may want to add.*

TO SUM IT UP

From what we have just been saying there is every reason to believe that a practical and even distinguished pageant can be put together from either a ready-made script or a custom-built one by a group of relatively theatrically inexperienced people. However, they must follow the rules which we have laid down. They must have an action scenario suitable to the actors obtainable, the money available, and the place of presentation selected. They must have a theme, a basic action scenario, appropriate narration to accompany the scenario, and a musical and sound plot.

A group of writers, perhaps each handling a different scene, if they

"Independence!" Episode 1 - Scene 1

NARRATION	TIME	ACTION
1st NARRATOR (Modern): Philadelphia, July 4th, 1776. The day began like any other day . . . (Pause) . . .	2 Minutes + 20 Seconds	Watchman enters upper right.
WATCHMAN: Six o'clock and all's well. (Repeats ad-lib) . . .	4 Minutes	Walks slowly from lamp to lamp, turning out lights, ringing bell.
2nd NARRATOR (Yankee Doodle): The night watchman made his rounds . . .		Drunks & Trollops enter upper left. Come down stage singing, bump into Watchman, etc.
Those who have spent the night carousing go home. The working people go to open their shops. They take their politics seriously.	6 Minutes	Workmen drift in all entrances, greet each other - some peer into Independence Hall windows, some argue. Tension mounts. 4 Redcoats march by.
2nd NARRATOR: For months the Continental Congress has been debating here about unfair taxation. Appeals to King George III have gone unanswered.	6 Minutes	Vendors enter, all entrances, ply wares. Schoolboys enter upper & lower right. Play leapfrog & other games.
WATCHMAN: Seven o'clock and all's well. (Off-stage) . . . Seven o'clock and all's well.	7 Minutes	Farmer backs wagon onstage down right. Exit Watchman upper left. Farmer unloads produce. Colonial soldiers enter & stand around.
2nd NARRATOR: A rumor runs through the streets. Yesterday the Virginia Delegation brought in a startling proposal - INDEPENDENCE!	7 Minutes	Vendors with carts, etc., from all entrances, fill stage. Carpenter & Tanner fight. Crowd watches.
1st NARRATOR: Philadelphia goes to market.		German Band enters, breaking up fight.
2nd NARRATOR: How will the Congress vote?	7 Minutes	Ladies with Servants enter & shop. Gentlemen come on from all entrances, greet Ladies, gather in groups, argue. Animated street scene.
1st NARRATOR: Here come the members of the Congress. (He identifies them as they enter). 2nd NARRATOR: Will these men cut the ties that have bound us to our mother country? Do they dare defy King George? Will the 13 united colonies become the United States? (He describes Jefferson, Franklin, J. & S. Adams & others).	10 to 15 Minutes	Hancock enters in coach, with Liberty Boys. Delegates enter in pairs, in groups, alone. Some speak to citizens, some join each other. Gradually exit into Independence Hall thru center door. The crowd is impressed. The Delegates are serious & intent on the business of the day. Following their exit . . .
	4 Minutes	Animated street scene resumes.

A Page of the Rehearsal Script for *Independence!*

"Independence!" Episode 1 Scene 1

CHARACTERS	MUSIC & SOUND
Fife & Drum Corps 1st Narrator (Modern Dress) 2nd Narrator (Yankee Doodle)	Fifes & Drums - a bright patriotic air Morning sounds. A cock crows, birds sing. Bell tower strikes <u>Six</u>. Distant chorus (off-stage).
Watchman Drunks & Trollops .	Watchman's bell. Drunks & Trollops sing bawdy ditties.

Workmen: Carpenters   4 Redcoats, 1 is a
        Tanners   Sergeant
        Tinkers   1 Redcoat Drummer Boy
        Weavers, etc.
	Some Workmen whistle.
	
	Drum.

Vendors: Kitchen Utensils, Pies & Cakes
       Cloth, News Broadsides, Flour,
       Toys, Flowers, Fans & Notions, etc.
Schoolboys & School Master
	Vendors' street crys.
	
	Schoolboys shout & cut up.

Farmer with fruit & vegetable cart Squad of Continental Soldiers, 1 is a Sergeant. Street Urchins following Soldiers	Tower bell & Watchman strike <u>Seven</u>. Soldiers sing in close harmony.
German Band Ladies of Quality with Maids & Liveried Servants. Gentlemen of Quality	Vendors' hawking & Crowd babble continues. German Band plays. Crowd applauds & sings along. Band & street crys continue. . . Liberty Boys - sing. Then <u>Tacit</u>. . . Silence - only Narrators' voices heard.
John Hancock & Liberty Boys. His Coachman (on foot). Delegates including Jefferson, Franklin, J. & S. Adams, etc. Congressional Sergeant at Arms & Clerks	
	German Band strikes up again. Street noises resume. Tower clock strikes <u>Eight</u>.

A Page of the Rehearsal Script for *Independence!* *(Cont.)*

have been well briefed on the historical background and well organized, can come up with a dramatic and appropriate script. Moreover, they must remember that small pageants can be as effective as large ones if they are simple, direct, and uncomplicated. Amateur pageants are largely dependent for their impact on the sincerity and naturalness which nonprofessionals bring to acting in place of a slick technique.

The simpler the pageant, the more necessary that it be written and produced with a thorough understanding of the available resources. The difference between a successful blockbuster and a successful modest production lies only in the size and the cost.

To repeat a word of caution already sounded, it is necessary that the writers, whether professional or amateur, recognize the limitations under which their brainchild will be produced. In all theatrical undertakings changes are almost certain to be made during rehearsals. It is during these that unexpected talents or limitations of actors and acting are revealed, and it is paramount that writers be willing to cooperate with the director in making changes.

But these changes should be within the skeleton of the script itself. Narration can be added or shortened. A musical number may have to be inserted or deleted. Bits of action may be discovered. To illustrate, in the 175th anniversary pageant just described, during a rehearsal a few of the boys on stage began playing leapfrog. This lively and colorful innovation was immediately incorporated in the scene with the school children. In addition to enlivening the scene, it gave individual actors standout parts and a sense of creation, but it didn't change the flow of the scenario. It is bits like this that lend charm to pageants and a good director has his antennae out to catch such things.

However, there must be a deadline for changes, even those made during rehearsal, and there must be a deadline for casting and costume-making. All technical details depend on that script and no rehearsal can get started until that valuable manuscript is in a usable condition.

8 Fitting the Music Into the Script

IN A PAGEANT, music is important in providing background or in setting the mood of the action. Here is where a good music director proves his worth.

THE MUSIC DIRECTOR

As work on the script goes forward, the music director gets into the act, for he will help make the decisions as to what and how much music to use and where it will be integrated into the script. A famous Hollywood producer, William Le Baron, once said, "When in doubt, use music." And it is true that the addition of music, either as background or as played or sung by the actors themselves, can certainly enhance the general effect.

A good music director has, of course, made himself familiar with the music of the period. In many cases this music has been preserved only as a single melodic line and must be "arranged"—scored for voices or instruments—before it can be used in the pageant. If the music director is not able to compose these arrangements himself, perhaps with the help of the recruiting and casting committee chairman (see Part IV), he can find somebody through a TV or radio station, or in a school or college music department who can do it for him.

In any case, the music director will have to prepare a whole music script, complete with cues, parallel to the written script so that he can synchronize the music with the action and narration. In the director's script, under a column headed "Sound," the music cues must also be set down (see the reproduction of one page of a rehearsal script in the preceding chapter).

The music script will include all the selections played or sung by bands, choruses, or soloists on the stage or behind the scenes, and a complete musical background played either by an orchestra in the pit, or, if the music director prefers, recorded on tapes or records. A word of warning: while recorded music may be easier to get and more professionally interpreted than that of a live, pickup orchestra, it is also more difficult to synchronize a mechanical device with stage action than to work with a live, adaptable conductor who understands what you're doing. *Moreover, if the music director wishes to use recordings or tapes or anything that has been copyrighted (including arrangements), he must have specific permission to do so from the copyright owners.*

MUSICAL GROUPS

The introduction of musical groups into the stage action is a device that contributes a great deal to the variety that we so desire in our pageant. A group of patriots coming on to the stage singing "Yankee Doodle" or "Bunker Hill" or "Chester" can be the high point of the scene. We have already described how the Liberty Boys sang as they pulled John Hancock's coach onto the stage at the 175th Anniversary Pageant at Philadelphia. Many of the songs that have come down to us mirror special conditions of the period, and can well be used. Brass bands were very popular in Revolutionary times; they included all types of horns and even whistles and flutes. Indeed, the flute was extremely popular among amateur musicians of the period (Thomas Jefferson played the flute), as were recorders. Recorders, being easier to play, were less exclusive, and someone playing a recorder can be introduced into almost any scene. For example, a group of school children on stage playing recorders might create a charming incident. Or there might be an impromptu street dance with music by strolling players. They could be playing woodwinds, brasses, or almost any kind of strings, modern or ancient.

SPECIAL MUSICAL EFFECTS

Highly recommended is the use of fanfares to highlight dramatic moments. Even kids in the school band can easily learn to play fanfares. To illustrate the extreme flexibility of this kind of thing, at a big Army show in a steel town, Ferde Grofé used the magnificent military brasses for martial effects, mounting his trumpeters on the highest tier of the arena *behind* the audience. On the other hand, at a ceremony at the Peace Light in Gettysburg, the Fanfare Group of the Valley Forge Military Academy, their long silver instruments gleaming in the sunshine and their music echoing across the fields, were equally thrilling.

As dramatic rehearsals proceed, these special musical effects should be integrated little by little. For this reason it is desirable that almost from the very beginning the music director should attend the rehearsals for actors. As early as possible, he should have a rehearsal pianist so that the actors get used to the music as they go along. As soon as his groups are sufficiently trained, they also should attend the acting rehearsals. But they should not come until they are sufficiently familiar with their routine, so that they will add to instead of disrupt the rehearsals.

As soon as possible the pianist should play the accompanying offstage musical score. For it is necessary that the score should cover the action and the music director may find it necessary, as the rehearsals develop, to add or subtract material from his score. And the only way he can find out what is necessary is to watch the action as it develops in rehearsal.

HELP FOR THE MUSIC DIRECTOR

The music director will probably find that he needs some assistants to carry out his program. In addition to the rehearsal pianist, he may have to find bandleaders, an orchestral conductor, and somebody who can train choruses, or somebody to arrange the music and compose any original bits and pieces that may be added. Indeed, he may find himself more of a chairman of a group than a one-sided music director.

The budget must contain ample provision for getting this work done. Copying music, for instance, costs money, and it is important that the music director have in his hand, as soon as possible, a complete cue sheet of the whole production.

Suggestions of specific music and where to find it will be found in Part VIII, Sources and Resources, under Music.

Part IV

○○

THE
BACKSTAGE CREW

9 The Committees
and Their Work

WE HAVE ALREADY DISCUSSED the backstage specialists, the commanding officers in our production army. Now is the time to consider the backstage workers, the unsung privates who handle the glamorless but very essential tasks.

IMPORTANCE

A local toastmaster at a testimonial dinner once opened his speech with the following sentence: "We want to thank those people who contributed so much to the success of our enterprise by not being seen on stage."

Sounds funny, but his heart was in the right place. The people who are not seen and don't get the applause are just as important as the actors who come before the audience. Indeed, before any rehearsals begin, there are certain committees which must be set up. They are our guarantee, our ace-in-the-hole. These people should be recruited and should be functioning, more or less, not more than twelve weeks or less than ten before opening date. If you set these committees up too soon, they won't have any work to do, and they'll soon lose interest. But once you see the work of the steering committee on the way to completion, the budget estimated, and the script in an understandable state, the steering committee should get busy and appoint backstage committees. The best way to do this is to get good chairmen for special committees and let them help the chairman of community cooperation recruit their own assistants.

RECRUITING AND CASTING COMMITTEE

The chairman of this committee first of all must be a person of similar character to the chairman of community cooperation. He might even be the same person. Before he can go to work he must have an approximate cast of characters from the scriptwriters and the director. This cast of characters must include not only the principals but the bit players and everybody else as well. His committee need not be large, but it must be as diversified as possible. Ideally, it should be composed of people whose regular jobs bring them in contact with possible performers: a teacher, for instance, who may have coached school plays, or will know from classroom work which of her students have a flair for self-expression; or a lawyer who knows which other lawyers in his group have good presence and can speak well. In one re-enactment of the signing of the Declaration, for example, all the signers were recruited from the Bar Association. This not only gave a feeling of reality to the characters (so many of the actual signers were lawyers) but meant that the actors themselves had the ability to speak clearly and authoritatively some of the authentic lines of the meeting. They alternated with the narrator, who on this occasion was John Daly, then of "What's My Line?"

Another source of performers might be the radio-TV stations, since in small communities they frequently recruit non-professional actors to do bit parts and appear on panels. So they are likely to have a list of people who know how to behave when appearing before the public.

Of course, there are almost always Little Theater or college groups, and very often clubs, churches, and service clubs who put on shows. All sources should be tapped for participants.

The best kind of casting for amateurs is what is called "type casting." As an example, the real mayor of Gettysburg played the part of the burgess of the town who greeted Lincoln. An ex-governor of the state played the wartime governor. A popular preschool teacher shepherded the children who were her daily pupils; this group in the pageant, in costumes which they and their own mothers had concocted from designs by the designer, presented flowers to Lincoln when he came off the train at the station. These actors had no trouble interpreting their parts; they simply played themselves.

When he invites people to play in the pageant, the casting chairman should avoid, if possible, assigning them to a special part. This is so that the director and the writers can juggle things around, if they wish, when the cast shows up for the first rehearsal; for it is the director and the writers who know best the type of character they seek to create, and they will be influenced by personal preferences.

It's risky, for instance, to invite somebody to be Benjamin Franklin and when he shows up, to find that he would be a much better John Adams. Or that he turns out to be incapable of taking a principal part at all and must be changed into somebody with as big a name but less to do. In a word, the casting chairman, the committee, and those who are writing and actually putting on the pageant must work in closest cooperation from the very beginning. It's great if they can get a look at the chosen person, even before rehearsals are called, for it's very hard to change someone around publicly. In addition, people very often turn up at rehearsals who have been overlooked beforehand, and it's a good policy, wherever possible, to include them in the show. Sometimes these strays turn out to be, surprisingly enough, the stars.

Practically none of this work can be done until the writers have given the casting chairman a more or less firm list of pageant characters. And that list must be in his hands not less than eight weeks before the performance date.

BACKSTAGE WORKERS

Actors aren't the only people the casting chairman recruits. A good chairman will stand ready to assist all other backstage chairmen to get the right people for their own particular needs.

The backstage workers fall into two general categories: those who work on things actually used in the pageant and those who are in the backstage managerial positions. In the first category we have the costume committee, scenery and property committee, lighting and sound committee, and music committee. These people work with the designer, the technical director (who may also be the designer), the music director, and the production stage manager, whose special duties we will consider later in Part IV.

In the second category we have the rehearsal chairman (working with the production stage manager), the publicity assistant, who works with the general publicity chairman on matters especially having to do with cast and events at rehearsals, a company manager (assistant to the finance chairman), and a secretary-typist.

The people in the first category must be recruited early in the game and there should be a chairman of each committee. As soon as the scriptwriters can furnish a cast of characters, they should swing into action. Immediately thereafter the personnel of the second group should be ready for work, at least two weeks before rehearsals are to be called.

GENERAL INSTRUCTIONS FOR BACKSTAGE WORKERS

Things used on the stage are quite different in construction from those used in everyday life. On the stage the important thing is to create an *illusion*. It's just a waste of time to be meticulous with detail.

A piece of scenery, for instance, is never viewed from underneath or behind. On the stage you can use rough wood that no self-respecting carpenter would touch, but it must be strong for it is going to have a good deal of pushing around. It can't be sloppy, since things used in the theater take a real beating and must be of sturdy construction. But what we need most for scenery and artifacts is imagination and style.

It's the same with costumes. It's the shape of the design and the fit and not the size of the stitches or the quality of the fabrics that make a costume. Many a costume is improved at the last moment by the judicious use of safety pins (but be sure to use black safety pins, as the other kind catch the light and can be seen by the audience).

The rules are always the same. What we're after is an effect. Of course, this is easier to achieve if the show is at night under lights and the designer and the lighting men know their business. But it's absolutely necessary under any circumstances.

Even the most un-style-conscious woman knows today that there is a difference between the cut of an "A" skirt and of a circular skirt—the difference between fashion and dowdiness. This is even more true of a hoop skirt. A full skirt will never take the place of a properly cut hoop skirt, for a full skirt simply can't hang right. Period clothes for women are distinguishable by their basic shape. An eighteenth-century bouffant, for instance, is cut differently from a Civil War hoop skirt. And what is *under* a woman's costume is just as vital in making it hang right as the skirt itself. No matter how many ruffles you put under a full skirt, it won't take the place of a hoop. In all women's clothes, the lining and the underwear are just as important as the dress itself. What isn't seen by the audience in a woman's costume matters just as much as what is seen.

COSTUME CHAIRMAN

In order to have a good costume committee, you have to have a good costume chairman. His first job is to recruit the people for his committee. Perhaps he doesn't know how to do any of the actual work, but he must see that it gets done. His second is to recruit people to work with the designer, to allocate them to different tasks and to see that they carry out their assignments. It is he who will sign up the people who are to attend early rehearsals to get actors' measurements. If costumes are to be rented, he will work with the designer and the treasurer in making the contract with the costume house, being sure that a clause is included as to date of arrival. He may have to arrange for trucking the costumes, and he must be sure that he allows for emergencies in the budget. In a way, he is the "Simon Legree" of the production, at the same time (hopefully!) retaining his popularity.

One of the best ways for him to make friends and influence people is to look after the special interests of his backstage group. He must keep them feeling that they are making an important contribution. He must see that the publicity chairman lists all their names on the program. He might suggest to the director that the members of the costume committee should make costumes for themselves to be worn on the big night in the finale. This is a device that can be very successful. The more people who take part in the finale, the better it looks, and since the costume committee has been working in close connection with the staging, they can, with only a few rehearsals, take part in the grand exit march. This brings them before the audience and makes them feel like actors and not merely like invisible Brownies.

There is another gimmick a costume chairman can put into his agenda. It's very likely that his group will work at odd hours, and as they get nearer and nearer to performance time, these hours will get longer and longer. He should try to put a modest amount in his budget for light refreshments for his sewing and fitting assistants. Nothing seems to keep them more willing to work long hours than an occasional coffee break.

He should be allotted a petty cash revolving fund from the budget (see Backstage Treasurer) to take care of the inevitable unforeseen missing items—safety pins or a quarter of a yard of material to let out a waistline under a shawl or fichu. Or buttons. Or a glove that has disappeared. And nothing vanishes so quickly as scissors!

The costume chairman arranges for the space not only for *making* the costumes but for the actors to dress in. Rods or racks must be installed where the costumes will hang. There must be proper containers for bonnets, gloves, and hand props, and plenty of labels for the actors' names.

The working place of the costume committee should not be changed about. The best space for them to meet is a school gymnasium, a large hall, or a church auditorium. Workers for each episode or group should be given a definite spot of their own.

Another way of arranging things is to divide the hall into separate sections for making the same things. For instance, one group might be

"Independence!" Episode 1 - Scene 1

COSTUMES	PROPS
Fife & Drum Corps - Penn. Line brown, buff & white uniforms. Black tricorns, white trim.	Fifes & Drums.
1st Narrator - Contemporary dark business suit. 2nd Narrator (Yankee Doodle) - Colonial suit, red, white & blue chest sash & red, white & blue cockade & plumes on black tricorn. Watchman - a braid trimmed greatcoat & tricorn. Coat has shoulder capes. Drunks - Colonial suits, some a bit disheveled. Trollops - Colonial dresses, a bit loud & vulgar. Too many frills & feathers.	Bell & Lantern Some carry bottles. Some carry fans.
Workmen - homespun Colonial dress. Some have leather or canvas aprons. Very few coats, mostly rough work vests & breeches. No bright colors. Redcoats - British Colonial regimental uniforms. Vendors - similar to Workmen, but a shade or two brighter in color. Some have Colonial coats. Schoolboys - beige, brown & gray britches, vests in assorted muted colors. Very few jackets. Most wear black or gray tricorns. School Master - severe gray Quaker suit & hat.	Tools appropriate to their trade. Accoutrements but no muskets. Drum for Drummer Boy. Merchandise trays & goods appropriate to their trade. Some have books in straps or shoulder satchels. Bible & switch.
Continental Soldiers - Colonial blue & buff regimental uniforms. Urchins following Soldiers - similar to school boys, but poorer. Some are ragged & patched. Some in hand-me-downs which don't fit. Farmer - smock & straw tricorn. German Band - makeshift militia, a cross between uniforms & Penn. Dutch farm costumes.	Muskets & full accoutrements. Some have wooden swords and muskets. Cart, fruit & vegetables. Maybe a crate of poultry. Band instruments.
Ladies of Quality - fine, tasteful Colonial dresses & hats. Pastel colors, stripes & floral patterns. Servants - Men Servants in liveries. Maids in plain Colonial dresses, some wear aprons. Gentlemen of Quality - Elegant but plain Colonial suits, some with brocade vests & coats. All wear tricorns, most in black, some in grays.	A few carry parasols. One might ride in Sedan Chair. Assorted shopping baskets & packages. Some carry straight dress canes.
Hancock - elegant Colonial dress suit. Traveling cape & tricorn. Plum would be a fine color. Hancock's Coachman - full livery. Liberty Boys - assorted Colonial suits. All wear red, white & blue sashes, & cockades in tricorns. Delegates - Earth color Colonial suits. Well dressed but not elaborate. Predominant colors- gray, gray-blue, olive, brown, russet, beige & black. Congressional Sergeant at Arms - blue & buff livery. Braid trimmed tricorn. Clerks - plain black & gray Colonial suits.	Elegant leather document portfolio. Coachman's whip. Jefferson carries document - the Declaration of Independence. Some Delegates carry papers. Franklin has his spectles & cane. Sergeant at Arms carries staff or mace of office. Clerks have portfolios & papers.

Designer's Costume, Prop, and Makeup Chart for an Episode in _Independence!_

MAKE-UP	SPECIAL REMARKS
Fife & Drum Corps - some are old men, some are boys.	
1st Narrator 2nd Narrator (Yankee Doodle) Watchman - middle aged & pink. Drunks - some red noses, a few look ill. Trollops - high key theatrical make-up.	Could very well be Black. A jaunty, unpompous type. Florid, fat & self-important. At least one is very fat.
Workmen - leather beaten & rustic make-ups. Redcoats Schoolboys - a healthy freckled lot. School Master - pale, severe and aged.	Some are Black. Lean military types except for chubby Sergeant. A few are Black.
Continental Soldiers - they look like they've been thru the mill. Urchins - some dirty faces. Farmer - a healthy bumpkin. German Band - robust peasant types.	A few have head bandages or arms in slings. Some are Black. Some are Black. Some crated geese or chickens will add to his bit.
Ladies of Quality - generally pale. They don't go out in the sun often. Many have powdered wigs. Servants - able bodied types. Well fed. Gentlemen of Quality - some are young dandies, some portly, substantial merchants & lawyers, etc. Many have powdered wigs.	Some are Black.
Make-up of principal Delegates must be carefully researched from color portraits. (Stuart, Trumbell, Peale, etc.). They must accurately resemble characters they play, especially Jefferson, Hancock, Franklin, J. & S. Adams, etc. Congressional Sergeant at Arms Congressional Clerks - generally pale, careworn and under-nourished make-ups.	A small, intense man. He feels he's more important than Jefferson - or Washington for that matter. One or two Clerks might be Black. At least one is a tottering ancient.

Designer's Costume, Prop, and Makeup Chart for an Episode in *Independence!*

(Cont.)

making all the fichus or shawls or collars, another making all the hoops, and so on.

As early as possible the costume chairman should see that all parts of individual costumes are assembled. For example, as our shawl makers finish a shawl, it should be placed with the costume with which it belongs, preferably on a special hanger or in the container under the rack. He should see that a few extras of each small object are made and kept in a sort of central "disaster account." This is because in spite of all precaution, little things always get lost or misplaced. When this happens there is always this treasure chest of extras to fall back upon.

He should also set up a central "security officer" who keeps the needles, pins, tape measures, and petty findings and hands them out as they are needed. Remember, it's the little things that add up to big bills.

If one large place is not available, and several smaller places must be used, the same technique of separating finished costumes, episode by episode, must be strictly held to.

There is one difficulty with a big hall that can be easily overcome. Although professional stage people have practically no inhibitions about mixing the sexes, the less sophisticated amateurs, men and women and boys and girls, may object to being fitted in full view of each other. With this in mind, the costume chairman should borrow a few screens to divide the sexes. However, if this is carried so far that the men object to being fitted by women, the chairman should put his (or her) foot down.

When the time comes for the actors to be made up, the chairman should allot a space at one side of the hall where the makeup people can do their work. This won't happen until about a week before the actual performance, and by this time most of the costumes will be in place and the sewing people won't need so much room (see Makeup Committee below for further details).

Experience has taught that the job of the costume chairman is so diverse that he must appoint a small group of sub- or cochairmen: a very expert seamstress to oversee the sewing, a tailor to keep an eye on the men's costumes, a beautician to supervise the makeup, someone very meticulous for the props, and so on. These subchairmen, however, should also be actual workers. One must be careful not to have too many chiefs and not enough Indians.

COSTUME COMMITTEE

The designer makes the designs and the costume committee does the actual work of carrying them out.

Here's a committee which, unlike other committees, should be a large one. It should be made up first of all of people who know how to fit, sew, and cut. Mothers of the cast make fine costume committee members. If there are any tailors in town, try to get them to serve on this committee. They know how sleeves should fit and pants should hang. If only one tailor is available, make him a sort of subchairman (see preceding section) so that he can help the people making and fitting the men's costumes.

In men's period costumes well-fitting accessories do the trick. Sleeves that are put in clumsily and breeches that don't fit well around the calf of the leg are dead giveaways. A clever designer can simulate a velvet coat or jerkin by painting on canvas, but the neckwear, the sleeves, and the bottom of the pants or breeches must fit. Sloppy, ill-adjusted stocks, sleeves that are too long or too short, unsnug knees, and badly fitting wigs can ruin any costume, destroy any illusion, and make any scene laughable. It doesn't make any difference how well the neckwear is cut and stitched. It must be *put on* correctly, stylishly, and above all, neatly. And it takes an experienced person to do this.

Then we need dressers. They will see that the actors put their clothes on right, that they don't forget anything, and that they return whatever they have been wearing to their proper places after they are used. Teenagers of both sexes are good dressers if properly supervised by the designer and the fitters.

Important persons on the costume committee are the shoppers. There is always a good deal of shopping to do, especially at the last minute. (And don't forget those safety pins!)

All actors must be measured for their costumes and it takes two people to do this job, one to measure and one to write it down. The chairman of the costume committee can sign up two members of his committee to attend early rehearsals and get the measurements. This is the only way to get measurements, a few at a time, since the cast will be divided into small groups for early rehearsals. And since the measurements should be taken as soon as characters are chosen so that the actual work of making the costumes can go forward, this is the most efficient way to simplify a horrendous job. Taking measurements is a time-consuming and unglamorous necessity.

It goes without saying that sewing machines must be rented, begged, borrowed, or stolen, for the use of the costume committee.

RENTED COSTUMES

In a historical pageant it is almost certain that some of the costumes will have to be rented, especially character costumes, like those for Benjamin Franklin, John Adams, and John Hancock. Costumes are rented by the day; so it is expensive to have them delivered more than a day or two in advance of the performance. In all the author's years of experience, she has never seen a trunkful of rented costumes arrive that didn't need some alterations, especially to the sleeves, the necklines, and the knees in men's costumes, and the waists, necks, and hang of the women's costumes. And they always must be pressed.

Therefore, any locally made costumes must be finished, tried on, altered, and hanging neatly in place at least a week before the performance. This leaves the last few hectic days for individual fittings and rented costumes.

As mentioned previously, both the designer and costume committee chairman must be familiar with contracts.

When a trunkful of rented costumes arrives, they should be unpacked carefully and checked against the list which the costume house has sent. Each belt, musket, shoe buckle, fan, hat, or wig must be carefully noted so that it can be accounted for when the trunk is repacked. There is nothing more expensive than replacing rented accessories, and some of them like belts, boots, and muskets are irreplaceable. Besides which, you will find that a sufficient number of small items like stocks, fichus, and underskirts are not there. And the costume committee has to get busy at once and make them. Only rent those costumes that are absolutely unmakable, for half the fun of doing a pageant is creating the costumes. Of course, there are always certain items in period costumes that can't be made, like the leather belts and muskets mentioned. But in any case, every rented item should be checked and double-checked. A bill for replacing missing items can make hash of the best-made budget. The names of some reputable costume rental houses are listed under Rentals in Part VIII.

MAKEUP COMMITTEE

The makeup committee is a special section under the costume chairman. In these days it isn't difficult to find people of all ages and sexes who know something about the handling of makeup. They need only come to work about a week before the production. Their first meeting should be with the designer. He will point out to the makeup artists the difference between street and stage makeup, reminding them that, like the scenery, theatrical makeup is primarily for effect, and can be a good deal more slapdash and un-detailed than daily makeup. All of us have seen types whose makeup is so obvious that it wouldn't even do for the stage. In fact, they look as though they could go before a movie camera without any further adornment. This is not what we want. Of course, if the production is in the daytime, the makeup has to be more carefully done than that under artificial light.

The designer should give the makeup artists sketches or pictures of historical persons who are to appear in the pageant so they gain experience in copying real characters.

It's well for the designer to hold a few extra sessions of his makeup committee. At these times they practice on each other while he comments. They should learn also to adjust wigs and headdresses. Fortunately, the period of the Revolution was a period without beards, mustaches, and sideburns. This happily eliminates beard-growing contests as a part of the celebration. But if there *is* an episode in which these things are used, the makeup committee should have an opportunity to work with these too. Every now and then they may persuade an actor to offer himself as a model. Today's long hair is fine for the period.

It is mandatory that there shall be at least two rehearsals before the performance and one dress parade, at which time *every* actor in the cast must be made up. This is for timing as well as for accuracy.

PROPS AND SCENERY COMMITTEE

Props, scenery, and lighting personnel, just like the costume committee, are assistants to the designer. Since they won't have as many things to make as the costume committee, they can involve fewer people, but in any circumstance it is well to have a chairman each for props, scenery, and lighting, who will be responsible for getting the work done. For the prop committee, it is a good idea to enlist the help of someone who teaches arts and crafts, especially for the hand props. Do-it-yourself people, real carpenters and art students, are good sources for the membership of the scenery committee. For the lighting committee it is fine if you can discover professional electricians to do the work, although they are sometimes a little rigid in their ideas. Indeed, the people who work with the lights in the Little Theater, a janitor from a school auditorium, or a school or college handyman make splendid assistants.

As in the costume and makeup departments, these people will have to be briefed carefully on the difference between things made for ordinary use and theatrical technique.

Scenery in the conventional sense should be kept to a minimum. Indeed, it is best to have just one indefinite background that is always the same, the character of which is changed by large artifacts carried onto the stage by people in appropriate costume in full view of the audience. Outdoors no background scenery should be used at all, for what seems like a gentle wind causes riffles that destroy all semblance of reality.

Let me illustrate how scenery changes can be varied by the use of big artifacts. In one pageant we built a whole street in a stadium. The episode was an auction in which the plots of the original town were sold.

As the actors bid for certain lots by large visible signals such as raising their arms, the narrators explained what was going on. As each lot was sold, the narrators would say, "Today the _____ Company's building stands on that plot," and across the stadium would come one or two actors dressed as workmen carrying an oversized replica of a modern building. In this way, building by building was erected. At the end the main street of the town stood there.

Another good example was a pageant play done in Paris by the famous designer, Norman Bel Geddes. Here the scene required a fort. Men dressed as medieval soldiers came in procession, carrying what appeared to be great banners, and by arranging and rearranging themselves on the stage, they made a very effective suggestion of the battlements.

At one pageant where we needed the inside of the room in which the Constitution was adopted, the narrators explained that the caretakers of the hall were getting the place ready for the meeting. In came a corps of stagehands dressed as janitors who placed chairs and small tables in prearranged spots. The last things they brought in were the Chairman's desk and the famous chair in which Washington sat, recognizable by its high back decorated with what Dr. Franklin, in his memorable valedictory, described as "a Rising Sun." Having placed the furniture, the janitors dusted up and presto! there was the room in which the signing was to take place.

The audience was delighted to be party to the act.

This last device has been used several times, and in several different contexts—on a conventional stage, on a thrust stage, and once, on an outdoor platform in a big stadium.

In all of these cases the narrators should call attention to what is happening.

If in our Bicentennial Pageant, for instance, the front of our stage is being used for a street scene, and we want to set up a scene on an inner higher level of the stage, the narrator could be saying something like this: "While outside, the citizens of Philadelphia are going about their business, inside the hall, preparations are being made for the meeting where the adoption of a Declaration of Independence will be discussed."

While stagehands costumed as Colonial workers and merchants set up the inner stage, he might go on with an explanation. "The Congress has been meeting in this room for many months, all through the summer, but today the question of the Virginia Resolutions which call for independency is to be brought up, and a document will be prepared by Thomas Jefferson with the help of John Adams to be submitted for their consideration. . . ." And the whole time the inner stage is being set, and the actors on the forestage are continuing their activities in pantomime. The narrator may give an explanation of what the individual signers may be expected to do and perhaps even (if the stagehands need the time) describe what is going on in the Colonies—"General Gage has invaded Boston"—and so forth and so on.

In describing this technique the words "inner stage" and "forestage" have been used, and we have spoken about different levels on the stage. This creating of different levels on the stage is one of the most important jobs of the scenery committee. Since there is no formal scenery and practically no change of background, constructing the stage floor on different levels will add to visual variety. This irregularity can be attained by the use of platforms. If the pageant is held indoors in a school auditorium with the ceiling arch and a large apron or forestage, irregular platforms may be placed on the inner stage behind the arch. Then large scenes can be enacted on the forestage and small scenes can be pinpointed on different levels in back or "upstage." Even if the pageant is in a stadium, it is well to vary the floor level. A group of platforms can be placed at each end of the stadium, armory, or gymnasium, and smaller scenes can be emphasized by playing on them while the entire stadium surface is used for processions, dances, and gatherings of the citizenry.

Platforms like these are fairly expensive to build, but in almost every community, and certainly in every school, there are portable platforms that are used by choral societies or for sports events, band concerts, and the like. They can almost always be borrowed, though it takes a good scenery committee to round them up.

A clever designer can work out and an efficient scenery committee can construct a good variety of platforms from the material of a temporary grandstand.

LIGHTING AND SOUND

Lighting is also the province of the designer. If the pageant is going to be held at night, it must be lighted. One of the cardinal sins of Little Theater groups is that of inadequate lighting. Remember that the most important thing in a pageant is visibility. However, this is a relative term, and by having a variety of lighting, bright spots may seem brighter and color spots more intense. Almost every Public Athletic League or playground has lights that are available for use, and these kinds of lights, though less sophisticated than spots, are splendid for outdoor use. The lighting committee will, first of all, have to round up the equipment. If they have to augment it by renting, there are several good lighting houses in New York, Chicago, and Los Angeles that specialize in rentals. Consult the telephone yellow pages in the city nearest you, if you do have to get some spots or buy some color screens. The designer should tell you what colors he wants. You can even rent switchboards. Keep your rental to a minimum, however, for though the actual prices may seem moderate, shipping of this kind of material is quite expensive.

Lights can be installed in almost every case locally, under the direction of the designer. In some instances, I have found it possible to get the lighting men from the local theaters to help. This means that you either have to pay union rates, or get some kind of concession from the union before these people may work with amateurs.

However, in many Little Theaters there are people who have made a hobby of theatrical lighting and they are, though slightly less efficient, more understanding of dramatic problems. Be sure that your lighting is installed safely. Don't have exposed wires lying around where actors can trip over them. Cover them with some kind of insulating material that is entirely visible or paint your cables white. Actors who are thinking of their parts are very apt to trip over uncovered wires. The result, either an injured actor or a disconnected wire.

Lighting cues should be worked out by the director, the designer, and the stage electrician, and numbered. Each person who is going to work lights should have a cue sheet, on which appear the numbers and the cue on which that number should be turned on or off. For example, Number 4 might be spotlight No. 6 on John Adams. "Adams crosses stage and places his hand on the speaker's desk." Or, "John Adams stands up in place." The lights must synchronize with the action.

Keep your lighting as simple as possible. Like everything else, good modest lighting is better than fancy effects that are difficult to work and probably won't.

There are two aspects to the so-called use of sound. One is the question of amplification, the other is the more complicated one of using sound in multimedia—with pictures, perhaps. In any case, this branch of production should be handled by people who understand, first of all, the technical aspects. There are such people in TV and radio stations, in the movie houses, and very often there are people attached to schools, Little Theaters, and even libraries who understand putting in microphones and sound equipment.

The most important thing about amplification is to make it intelligible without making it too loud. Since most of the words that are spoken will be delivered by the narrators, who, we hope, are speakers with some training, this aspect doesn't present too many difficulties. However, make sure that the words can be heard and understood in every part of the house, stadium, or hall in which the pageant is given. Many school auditoriums are already wired for sound, and even stadiums sometimes have a loudspeaker system. If the pageant is held in such a place, the whole problem is simplified.

On the other hand, the problem of using pictures with sound gets more complicated, but there are many people today—teachers, travel fans, home movie addicts—who know a good deal about the use of multimedia and can be very helpful. But be sure, if you show pictures in connection with live action, that the actors' shadows don't show on the screen. And also be sure that the pictures can be seen from every part of the audience.

If you amplify the background music, keep it on a level that does not interfere with the narrators' voices whenever they are speaking. Bring it up only in the places where there is no narration. Singers and other musicians who come on stage present quite another problem. If possible, try them out beforehand, and make sure that amplification is absolutely necessary. Don't just use it. Use it only if it will improve the results you want. Sometimes a very good effect can be achieved by alternating amplification and the human voice.

Keep your microphones as invisible as possible. Nothing spoils an illusion so much as seeing a 1776 lady step up to a 1976 mike. An amplifier can be hidden on the floor and a chorus can gather round it without the action being too obvious. Be careful in all cases that the motion toward a microphone is not stilted.

In any case, amplification is a highly specialized and complicated business. Except in the case of the narrator, where it is almost invariably necessary, it should be kept to a minimum.

The sound committee should not consider their job done until they have the director's O.K.

MULTIMEDIA

This is a new word for the old idea of employing mechanical aids in dramatic presentations. Multi—many; medium—an agency, means, or instrument. It is used today to apply to the presentation of ideas through newspapers, radio, and so forth. In its broadest sense, the multimedia are used as teaching aids, dramatically to point up special situations.

The multimedia we talk about include lights, recorded sound, film clips, and motion pictures. In pageantry, the multimedia can be very helpful for backgrounds, environmental effects, dramatic emphasis, and bridges between scenes.

They must, however, be used with caution. They should be combined with the live part of the show, not substituted for it.

Because multimedia are being used widely as teaching aids, companies specializing in multimedia material are proliferating. Consult with someone in your schools, find out where they are getting their visual aids, and contact the company that is already dealing with your locality. Study its catalogues and see what will be useful to you in the way of sound effects, lighting effects, film clips, or motion pictures. Caution: Use them sparingly.

If you are going to throw anything onto a screen, be sure the screen is placed in such a way on the stage that the shadows of the actors are not reflected on the screen. It may be that a school in your vicinity has the apparatus for rear projection. If so, you are lucky. Or you may find such a machine in a television studio. Whoever operates the machine must be a skilful operator who understands the machine thoroughly, and who has rehearsed thoroughly with the live part of the show.

Never *substitute* a picture for live action; combine them.

Here is an example of the use of multimedia in a pageant that has already been presented.

HAYM SALOMON AND THE BATTLE OF TRENTON

Haym Salomon and George Washington are discovered downstage R. at a campfire in conference, picked up by a small spotlight. On a screen in the background is a snow scene at Washington's Crossing. The narrator explains that Washington needs supplies for his men, and especially money to buy boats for his secret expedition against Trenton. He has called in the Philadelphia financier, Haym Salomon, and appeals for help. Salomon promises to get it.

Spotlight off. Scene on screen changes to the interior of an Orthodox synagogue. It is the end of the Day of Atonement, Yom Kippur, the holiest day in the year. The Jews of Philadelphia are gathered in their synagogue awaiting sundown. On this day, no practicing Jew carries anything. Not one of them has a single penny, money purses have been left at home. Material possessions may not even be mentioned.

The sound of the men praying is drowned out in the sound of a storm, and a galloping of a horse's hoofs. Salomon appears onstage. Against his religious belief, he has ridden on this holy day.

The synagogue scene shuts off. Men (live actors) in praying shawls and yarmulkas swarm around Salomon protesting. This is all explained by the narrator. Why has Salomon interrupted this holiest of holy days in this sacrilegious manner? Salomon explains that Washington is desperate, he must have money at once or his army will melt away before he can strike another blow for freedom.

They ask him to wait for sundown, the narrator goes on. Too late, says Salomon, it's now or never. The Jews confer. Then they go offstage. A picture of the empty synagogue is thrown on the screen, and the narrator explains that they are going to their homes and will bring back money and supplies. A horse and wagon drive on the stage. The men of the congregation return, carrying packages or money bags which they pile into the wagon. Salomon drives off. The congregation leaves. On the screen we once more see the congregation praying, and over the sound of the storm we hear the ram's horn (the Shofar). End of the scene.

This is a detailed description of how to combine sound, light, pictures, and people in a realistic pageant scene. It's easy to see that everything has to synchronize, and that each element enhances the other.

In the case of more abstract treatments, sounds, noises, and, above all, music, can heighten effects. Suppose, for instance, you were showing the signing of the Declaration and you wanted to indicate that the framers were influenced by philosophers; their voices with echo effect could be heard expounding their philosophy, seeming to come from all around. Or in the case of a westward migration, the difficulties that the travelers encounter could be indicated by sound as well as music—Indians, storms, wild animals.

There are dozens of ways in which the multimedia can enhance a scene and enlarge the stature of the human actors taking part in it. The limitations are principally budgetary. But remember, don't get too abstract. The audience must understand what's going on.

10 Three More Backstage Notables

WITHOUT MINIMIZING the importance of the chairmen and workers whom we have just discussed, it is appropriate at this point to focus attention on three people whose work is special enough not to fit into the categories named in the preceding section.

PRODUCTION STAGE MANAGER

Before we call any rehearsals a "Gal Friday" (male or female) character must be added to the roster. This character is the production stage manager. He is the director's righthand man all during rehearsals, and after the curtain goes up, he is the boss. At this time, even if something goes wrong and the director sees the way to cover it, under no circumstances must he communicate directly with the performers, but must transmit the orders through the production stage manager. The production stage manager is supreme during dress rehearsal and performance. From the very beginning the actors must recognize his authority. Otherwise, the result is chaos.

Up to curtain time the production stage manager is the director's assistant. He gives out all rehearsal calls. He will notify the actors and make sure they are available. He announces the places for rehearsal, selecting them from the space already promised to the chairman for community cooperation.

The production stage manager will have assistant stage managers. A good plan is to assign an assistant stage manager not only to each episode, but to each group in an episode. These group stage managers are also actors in their own groups. Their interest is not merely in their own part but in the parts of the actors under their leadership. They wear costumes that harmonize so that they can move around freely on the stage without the audience noticing them. Indeed, it's practical to have *all* the technical people in costume, so that if anything goes wrong (and, alas, in amateur performances this often happens), one of them may step in without the knowledge of the audience.

The production stage manager will assign an assistant to be present at every rehearsal, and take part in his special scene. If someone is absent from rehearsal (and this is sure to happen when volunteers are involved) the assistant stage manager can take the absentee's part, and the rehearsal can go on without confusion. In other words, the assistant stage manager is the understudy for the actors in his group.

Let us suppose that a few special characters need extra rehearsals. Instead of calling the whole group, a stage manager can substitute for the missing characters. He can even represent missing artifacts. I remember very well a pageant put on by workers from the Weirton Steel Company, with Army personnel and equipment. At first, the workers were rehearsed by themselves, since the Army equipment and the people who used it were not able to come to rehearsals until just before the dress rehearsal. At the early rehearsals when the time came for these props to appear on the stage, the production stage manager and his assistants would come running in shouting "We are twenty jeeps" or "We are three helicopters." The first time this happened everybody had a good laugh. But in a few minutes they understood the practicability of this maneuver and were all prepared to play their parts when the actual jeeps finally came on the scene.

The stage managers will also have close association with the costume committee. Each stage manager must be thoroughly familiar with the costumes and props of every person under his jurisdiction. He must always see that each actor in his group has his or her hand props. In the early rehearsals the stage manager will have to use makeshifts. But it is his job to see that the makeshifts are there at each rehearsal so that the actors get used to using them.

A very good nontheater example of stage managerial responsibility was demonstrated by the men in the Houston Space Center during the Apollo 11 moon shot. Each one was looking after some tiny special aspect of the astronauts' movements, clothing, or equipment (the astronautic equivalent of costumes and props). To the TV watchers there seemed to be an unnecessary delay in opening the door from Eagle so that the first man could stand on the moon. Actually, that delay was planned so that the men in the Space Center at Houston could recheck with the astronauts every detail of their performance and costumes and props. And after the landing was made and the astronauts were ready to leave, it seemed that Armstrong was going to forget to pick up one of his props to take back with him. "Oh, I wouldn't have let him get away with that," said Don Lamm of Houston, in a subsequent interview. "I was all ready to remind him. But he remembered to go back and pick it up." In other words, Armstrong had been thoroughly rehearsed, and so had Lamm, his stage manager.

Special groups like choruses or bands that come on stage, or dancers, will have their own leaders who are *their* stage managers. They, too, are responsible to the production stage manager.

Stage managers have special duties, not only on stage and during the preliminary rehearsal period, but they are even more indispensable during the dress parade, dress rehearsals, and, of course, at the time of the performance. We will describe this in detail when discussing these special occasions. But in every case, they are responsible directly to the production stage manager.

It is essential that all of the stage managers keep in touch with each other, and with the leader of the orchestra. If your production covers a large area, this can be done by installing telephones with long cords (so that the stage managers are able to move around). Or, if this is impossible, by the use of radio telephones, which are a bit chancy. Stage managers must also be in touch with the orchestra director, for one never knows when a group is delayed for some reason or other, or an actor didn't show up, and a quick-thinking stage manager can change the order of things and cover up.

Telephones are preferable to other forms of communication, and they must all be open so that every stage manager and orchestra leader knows everything in case they can't see each other. Get your local telephone company to install the phones as a present. For the radio telephones—sometimes called "walkie-talkies"—the prime source is the

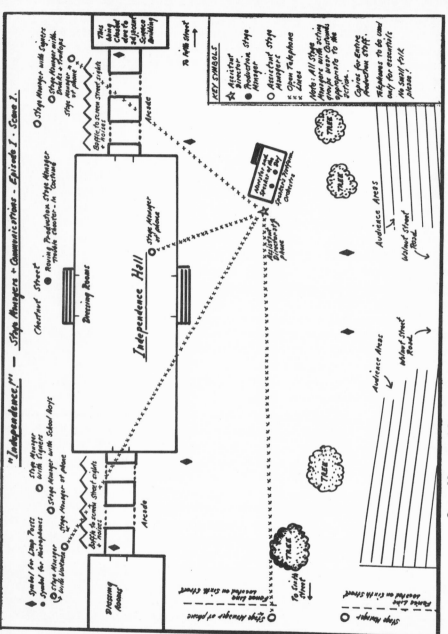

Stage Managers' Communications Lines for an Episode in *Independence!*

nearest military installation, or perhaps your television station can supply you.

If you are working in a small space you may have runners who will keep all the stage managers in touch with each other. The necessity of keeping in touch is very, very important, and cannot be too strongly emphasized.

Stage managers will find *The Stage Manager's Handbook,* listed under Backstage Management in Part VIII, helpful.

BACKSTAGE TREASURER

An essential person on the backstage committee is the treasurer. He is the representative of the financial chairman on the front of the house committee. It is he who handles the money that is used backstage, and keeps the accounts. He must have a flexible attitude toward his job and must be in thorough sympathy with the people who are spending the money. He must understand the needs of the different backstage groups. One of the most painful things that a treasurer has to do is to steal money from one activity and give it to another. He must stand ready and willing to do this at the request of the director. For example, if the script-writers need a little extra money for typing, he might discover a way to cut a corner in the publicity budget and allocate the money to the script-writers.

He must not, however, assume too much authority. But he must be willing to juggle things even when he doesn't understand them. At one pageant, for instance, we had a treasurer who hated to disburse money from the petty cash fund. It was he who asked plaintively, upon getting a bill for gelatins, why the actors had to be fed, and was only partly mollified when he discovered that a gelatin was a color screen for a light.

On the other hand, one treasurer saved the day by sending out on his own authority for soft drinks for the cast on a particularly hot night during a long and trying rehearsal.

If possible, the treasurer should have a secretary who is also the secretary to the entire backstage bureaucracy, and who runs the office, keeps the accounts, answers the telephone and, if volunteer help cannot be found, types up daily notes for the director and the designer.

The treasurer should always keep his eye on the budget and if more funds are absolutely necessary, he should stand ready to go with the director to the steering committee and act as advocate.

The treasurer for backstage should be appointed very early in the game. He might begin as an assistant to the finance chairman and graduate to backstage treasurer, as expenses for backstage begin to evolve.

Although the treasurer is responsible for these backstage expenses, he should not be involved in paying out fees, if any, for what professional staff may be engaged. The director should deal only with the chairman of the steering committee and receive his stipend, large or small, from the finance chairman. This goes also in case the steering committee, in consultation with the director, decides to employ a professional designer or music director.

All other backstage disbursements are the province of the backstage treasurer.

Of course, the treasurer will understand his overall budget and break it down for the record into its component parts—so much for rented costumes, so much for wigs and makeup, so much for materials and findings and lumber and petty cash. He must be prepared to discover that directors, designers, and such people really are often quite stupid about financial details, and he must be patient with their vagaries just as they must be patient with him in explaining their artistic needs.

A good backstage treasurer is a wonderful influence for harmony.

SPECIAL EVENTS CHAIRMAN

In addition to the overall publicity chairman, and working with him, it is well to have someone who is concerned entirely with backstage goings-on as a source of news. He should attend all planning meetings, all rehearsals, and look in frequently on the doings of the costume and scenery committees. In case he cannot do this by himself, he should create a very small committee to keep up with backstage doings. Something is always happening there that will make a good news story. The backstage special events chairman and his committee are the people who see, understand, and even create such stories, and feed them to newspapers, radio, and TV programs.

These inside stories of production activities make good publicity. Thumbnail sketches of participants, individual directors, and special chairmen can make news if properly angled. There's always something newsworthy going on in the costume committee and at rehearsals.

A good chairman of special events will think up ways to create news when things are in the doldrums; a constant flow of interesting items about the development of the pageant project is the only way of keeping the public anxious to attend the performance.

However, these squibs should be released only in consultation with the general publicity chairman. For he himself may have a story of his own that he decides should have preference, and he should make the decision as to which story comes first.

It is the chairman of special events, with the director, who compiles the cast of characters as it appears on any program. He must be especially careful that the names of participants are spelled correctly. There must be no mistakes in the final version. The form of each name must meet the approval of the person named. Many people have nicknames which they favor. Some Thomases prefer "Tom," some Johns prefer "Jack." Some Elizabeths have a fondness for "Elsie" or "Liz." On the other hand, a person who's known by a nickname may like to have his own name used. *Every person* concerned backstage should get proper billing, no matter how small and insignificant his job may seem. Being mentioned on the program gives ego-satisfaction and, as we have said before, helps guarantee an audience. Not only the committees, the cast, and the workers, but every person who has lent any object, even the least spectacular, must have a credit on the program.

This seems petty as we tell it, but billing is terribly important to those involved. It's a touchy matter—not only with amateurs. The proper spelling of names and the proper credits should be the first concern of every good newsman. Indeed, in some news media, a name misspelled also spells the exit of the reporter, and it is accepted as "dismissal for cause" by unions.

In the event that the steering committee has decided to have a souvenir program, this will have to be printed quite a while before the day of the performance. One of the uses of such a souvenir program is to mail it out.

Between the time of the going to press of the souvenir program and the actual performance, some cast changes will have been made and names added. Therefore it is a good idea to have, in addition to this more elaborate program, an inexpensive broadside or folder that can be loosely inserted in the official program, and on which corrections can be made at the last minute. This folder is the responsibility of the special events chairman.

11 Recapitulation

THE GROUNDWORK for our pageant is now well under way, and curtain time for the production is drawing near. The committees, the direc-

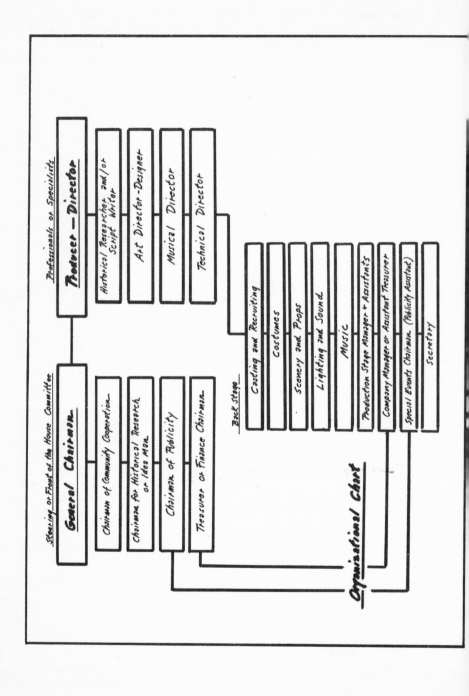

Organizational Chart

Professionals or Specialists

Producer — Director

- Historical Researcher and/or Script Writer
- Art Director - Designer
- Musical Director
- Technical Director

Steering or Front of the House Committee

General Chairman

- Chairman of Community Cooperation
- Chairman for Historical Research or Idea Man
- Chairman of Publicity
- Treasurer or Finance Chairman

Back Stage

- Casting and Recruiting
- Costumes
- Scenery and Props
- Lighting and Sound
- Music
- Production Stage Manager + Assistants
- Company Manager or Assistant Treasurer
- Special Events Chairman (Publicity Assistant)
- Secretary

tor, and the specialists have been doing their work steadily according to plan. They have a reassuring portion of the budget, either on hand or pledged, and have allocated it to front of the house or backstage, with a comfortable margin for the unexpected. They know where to look for further help if it is needed. The script is in workable condition, and a roster of actors has been established. Now our organization chart looks like the chart on page 94.

Like runners in a race our organization has been drawn up at the starting line "on their mark."

Now the business of rehearsals can get under way.

Let's "get set."

Part V

ooooooooooooooooooooooooooooooooooooo

THE FIRST
REHEARSAL

12 Rehearsal Call

NOT MORE THAN TEN WEEKS or less than eight, depending on the complexity of the production, the production stage manager sends out a call for the first rehearsal. The time for the meeting should be set only a few days after the invitations are received, so that the excitement will not die down. The invitations should be given in the name of the chairman of the steering committee, the casting chairman, the director, and the professional staff, all of whom will, of course, plan to be there. Working chairmen—costume, scenery, etc.—should also plan to be present. Their committees may come if they wish, in order to get the feel of the thing, but it is not mandatory on this occasion. And, of course, all potential actors will be there.

This will probably be the only time that a crowd as large as this will get together until shortly before the dress rehearsal. After the first meeting, episodes and even bits and pieces of episodes will be rehearsed separately, and then gradually brought together.

Pageant producing is like making a movie. Actors must know their own parts perfectly but they need have only a general idea of the rest of the show. Since we are dealing with volunteers, and must keep them interested, we are using this first rehearsal to introduce them to each other,

99

explain to them the parts they will play, and outline for them the over-all action, how it will be developed dramatically, and where their own special scene or episode fits into the picture.

This first rehearsal cannot be a haphazard affair.

13 The First Rehearsal

THE MANNER IN WHICH this first rehearsal is conducted will spell success or failure for all future rehearsals. The procedure must be care-fully worked out so that all the prospective participants who are coming together for the first time get a clear idea of the work that has already gone into the project and a graphic picture of what the pageant itself will be like, and what part they will play in it.

PLANNING

Every detail of the rehearsal must be planned before this first rehearsal. It must be remembered that a cast of amateurs has only a limited amount of time to give to rehearsal, time that they take off from their daily living. They also have only a limited amount of theatrical know-how and cannot keep on developing their parts the way professionals do. Because of this, they cannot absorb as many rehearsals as profession-als, and after they have reached the limit of their capabilities they are likely to get bored and go stale. Therefore, the people conducting the re-hearsals must know exactly what they are going to ask for.

There will, naturally, have to be a few preliminary remarks by the high-er echelon chairmen, but the real value of this meeting is an easily understandable presentation of the way in which the dramatic work of the next few weeks will be carried on, and how it relates to the people who have come to the meeting.

STAGE MOVEMENT

The designer has made a series of sketches representing the floor plans of the stage. These floor plans have been reproduced on sheets of card-board large enough to be tacked up on the wall and easily studied.

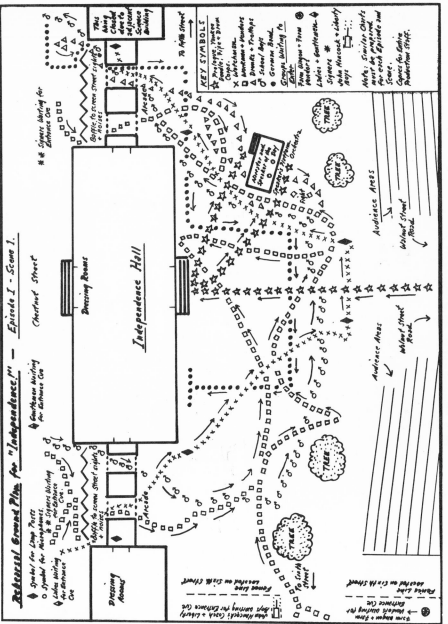

Floor Plan for an Episode in *Independence!*

There is at least one floor plan or stage plot for each episode. If there are subepisodes, more charts are needed. On each floor plan the director has plotted out, in different colored crayons, the movements of individual groups and characters in that particular scene. These charts or plans are easy to explain and fun to look at, and they make it possible for our assistant stage managers to conduct small rehearsals with actors understanding the general overall plan into which their action fits.

These charts, once made, are the particular responsibility of the production stage manager. He has been thoroughly briefed about the manner of using them and he understands in detail what they are all about.

After the first rehearsal he assigns them to the assistant stage managers in charge of particular episodes. At the end of each rehearsal they are carefully returned to the production manager, checked over, and kept together in a central place.

These charts must be ready for use at the first rehearsal.

MASTER SCRIPT

The director should have in his hand for the first rehearsal a master script from which he can have excerpts read to whet the interest of the people who come.

Actually, his master script is in the making, for during rehearsals he will have to pull it apart, as we have pointed out, to promote unexpected talents or allow for limitations of actors and the physical requirements of the stage itself. Also, when music and movement are added to the words, the acting-out of a scenario may take too long or be too short, and adjustments must be made.

The final master script, when it is finished (which will probably be the night of the dress rehearsal), will be full of pencilled amendments, intelligible probably only to the director, the production stage manager, and the assistant stage managers, each one of whom will have his own copy. Many directors not only make marginal notes but draw small floor plans with action indicated on their copies and small matchstick figures to show the dramatic action of special characters.

It is the skeleton of this master script that the director will bring to the first rehearsal.

CASTING FOR THE FIRST REHEARSAL

The casting chairman must be prepared at this first meeting to read a cast of characters. However, this is very incomplete, with principals only. As the rehearsals go on, more and more of even the so-called extras will become characters.

In his own mind the casting chairman has pretty well decided which actor will play which character. He has selected his principal actors hopefully from having seen them in other productions or because they resemble physically a special historical character. But they may turn out to be duds and he must leave the director an "out" in casting. This is a very delicate matter, as I have pointed out before, but tryouts for volunteers are simply not possible. Changes sometimes must be made after rehearsals start—and sometimes, alas, an incompetent cannot be got rid of. In the latter case it is best to "simplify" his role as tactfully as possible.

COSTUME SKETCHES

For this first rehearsal the designer should also prepare a few simple costume sketches. These need not be finished drawings, just suggestions that he can tack up on the wall next to his charts for the people at the meeting to look at. Very often when designers make costume sketches, they add little details—gloves, parasols, lanterns, tools, bouquets, and other hand props—which make characters more vivid to the actors and indeed often give ideas to the director. Very often, when he draws characters in a group, he fires the imagination not only of the actors, but the director as well.

In other words, the contribution of the designer in this first rehearsal makes what is said at the rehearsal more practical and enlivens the atmosphere, an object greatly to be desired.

NARRATORS

An additional bonus at the first rehearsal can be gained by holding a preliminary short meeting of the narrators. At this time several different parts of the pageant could be selected for them to read at the rehearsal so that when the time comes for them to do their bit, there will be no fumbling around. Instead, they will go to work with precision and knowledgeability and impress the newcomers with the quality of their work and the script.

Now we are ready to face our potential actors at the first rehearsal.

Stock - 2 fold-
ed + pleated
handkerchiefs

Practical Brass
Bell

Millinery felt hat fo
cut, sides tacked up
+ trimming added.

Old Surplus Army Coat.
Dyed. Shoulder cape, cuffs
& appliqued pocket flaps
added. Brass buttons +
rickrack braid.

Watchman
"Independence"

Practical Lantern
can be made from
small bird cage

Black loafers
Add buckles on
elastic.

Alfred Stern

Sew fringe hair to hat if boy has short hair

Head dress made from doily & ribbon bow.

All shoes black

School Children
"Independence"

Dirndl Dress
Add Apron
+ Trimming

Alfred Stern

Chef's hat cut down
Add lace + ribbon trimming

Dirndl Dress
with Matress Ticking
Panniers + Peplum
Lots of full
petticoats same
length as skirt

Ribbon + Lace
Border added

Lady of Quality
"Independence"

Black Shoes

Alfred Stone

14 Conducting the First Rehearsal

HOPEFULLY we have a sizable crowd at this first get-together. Of course, some people who were invited will be missing, but don't be discouraged; this is bound to happen. It is from this first rehearsal that the participants will get their impression—and they will pass it on to others—of whether it is going to be fun to take part in the pageant. The most important thing in this first rehearsal is to spark the interest of the people present. This can be done only if the meeting has been well planned. There must be absolutely no hemming and hawing.

PROGRAM FOR THE FIRST REHEARSAL

Hold your meeting in a large, comfortable place and be sure you have enough chairs for everybody.

Begin the meeting on time. You'll find at this first meeting that people keep drifting in, but if they see that the announced schedule has been strictly adhered to they will make the effort the *next* time to arrive at the hour indicated.

Open your meeting with a short welcoming talk by the executive chairman, not more than three minutes. He should give the group some idea of the importance of the production and what the promoters hope will be accomplished by it. Then he introduces someone who tells the story of the pageant. He must be very brief (not more than four minutes) and clear, and he may even read small parts of the script. It is preferable, however, that the narrators, already prepared, should do the reading, just for variety.

Next the casting director is introduced. Maybe he reads the entire cast of characters. He indicates who will take a few of the more recognizable parts (if they are present) and explains that even people without name parts are individual characters.

The whole procedure should take, at most, ten minutes. In order to prevent a group of amateurs from jumping up and down and visiting with each other, they must be kept constantly interested. Since acting in a pageant is not their main occupation, and the time they give to a rehearsal is taken off from their daily living, they must be made to feel that every moment they spend at a rehearsal is vital to the production.

After the explanatory part of the meeting, the director takes over. He repeats that the people present who are not assigned are people who have been chosen to perform in individual episodes. He introduces the special groups to their stage managers, and he introduces the designer. Perhaps this is a good place to introduce the costume chairman too.

The designer has brought with him the blowups, which we have explained, of the stage floor plot. He has put these around the room so that the people who come to the meeting can look at them. While he is talking, he should encourage his listeners to get up and examine the pictures. Keep them active! Don't let them feel that they are being lectured at!

Now that the meeting has become informal, the director should take over once more. This is the time for him to explain a little about the difference between everyday behavior and acting. He gets his prospective cast to practice some of the pointers he will give them in stage deportment. He illustrates the necessity of good muscular control by making them practice the techniques of sitting, standing, and walking. He demonstrates how one large gesture is worth half a dozen small ones on a stage. When an actor is pointing at something, he explains, he should point once and hold that position. Then and there, the actors are encouraged to make gestures so they can see for themselves what he means. They are also given some exercises in muscular control to be practiced at home. Of course, while all this is going on, there is a great deal of laughing, talking, and moving about, and it is in this relaxed atmosphere that the first rehearsal draws to a close.

The production stage manager gives the call for the next rehearsal. He sets the time and place and reads the names of those who are to report.

Rehearsal dismissed!

IMPORTANCE OF THE FIRST REHEARSAL

The attendance and the enthusiasm at all future rehearsals depend on how much the participants have enjoyed this first meeting. Their involvement can be obtained by observing certain rules. The meeting must begin on time. What is said and done at the meeting must be well planned beforehand, snappy, and interesting. And though it should be short, it must be long enough to make the people who came feel it was worth their while. A little over an hour would be the ideal length. Every person who comes must go away convinced that the project too is worthwhile, and that he himself is responsible for making it a success or a failure.

EVERYBODY IS SOMEBODY

Ego identification is a prime ingredient for a well-made pageant. Every person who is at the first rehearsal, whether a principal or not, must have a character to portray. In a well-managed and interesting pageant there are no extras and no mob scenes. Every person on the stage must be playing a role of his own.

I was allowed to see the most distinguished producer of pageants of our time, the great regisseur, Max Reinhardt, rehearsing the enormous extravaganza, *The Eternal Road*. To any other director, the majority of people in the cast would have been just extras or crowds. But Reinhardt gave to each person, even walk-ons, a name and a specific character. Each performer on the stage had to "do his own thing." Strangely enough, an actor who is creating a role seems to occupy more stage space than if he were just a zombie, and this specialization not only makes the scene more interesting but reduces the number of "live bodies" necessary to fill the stage.

It's a good thing to let actors invent the kind of characters they would like to play. In a very early pageant which I directed, one of the bit players suggested that she might be a young lady carrying a bird cage. This same character has popped up repeatedly in subsequent pageants.

Sometimes the ladies carry lovebirds, sometimes parrots, sometimes canaries. In all cases the actress herself has invented the story of *why* she was carrying the bird. One said she was a spinster who had nobody at home with whom she could leave her bird. One was a young lady carrying a present to her grandmother. One had just bought the bird and was taking it home. Each person that chose the Bird Lady, invented her own interpretation of her character, and made it interesting not only to herself, but to the audience. She also always had a wonderful time at rehearsals, building up her part.

A strange thing seems to happen to a person who has once invented a character. He never forgets it. Years after the event, when I can hardly remember that I even directed some celebration, some totally unfamiliar person in some wholly unrelated place will recall himself to me.

"I played a drummer boy in *Mr. Lincoln Goes to Gettysburg,*" said a bespectacled professor of history.

"I was the street boy that followed the band in the *Fair of the Iron Horse,*" explained Alan Schneider, the successful Broadway director.

"I was the naughty child who got on the 1832 locomotive when my mother didn't want me to," (also at the *Fair of the Iron Horse*) recalled Sargent Shriver, lately Ambassador to the Quai d'Orsay.

A blooming matron reminded me that she had played a little girl who carried some flowers to give to Lincoln at Gettysburg, "but I got separated from my parents in the crowd," she said, "and I was too shy to go and speak to him alone, so I kept the flowers all through the pageant until they wilted away." She must have invented the story all by herself for there certainly was no such character in the formal cast.

There is no limit to the creativity that can be evoked by this kind of approach. This is especially true in the preparation of a Bicentennial Pageant. Every participant should be encouraged to do some research on the kind of character that he is going to portray. Of course, Benjamin Franklin, John Adams, and Thomas Jefferson are well documented, but some of the lesser-known convention members were also exceedingly interesting people—Caesar Rodney, John Dickinson, Francis Hopkinson, to list a few. Nor do we have to confine ourselves to the principal actors. A carpenter and his apprentice in a street scene would be well rewarded to do a little digging into the status of carpenters in Philadelphia in 1776. They would find that the Carpenters' Union was the first union in the Colonies, that the meeting of the First Continental Congress, the precursor of the Congress that adopted the Declaration, met in Carpenters' Hall because that was the place where free speech was allowed.

Or a couple of Quakers might trace the history of nonbelligerency among the conservative Friends and the schism that resulted when a group of Free Quakers decided to support the Revolution. The actors might choose which kind of Quaker each was going to represent and a whole bit of theatrical side-play might result.

Schoolboys playing games in the street might be interested to know what games were played in that day.

There are innumerable instances of this kind of ego involvement that bring a freshness and a spontaneity to the performance of amateurs. Thus a whole educational pattern can be evolved from a dramatic performance. Indeed, the side effects of a dose of theater of any kind are often more lasting than the performance itself.

15 Horses, People, and Other Animals

BEFORE WE PLUNGE into the subject of more rehearsals, let us discuss how the idea of flexibility within the overall framework of the pageant script can be used to add color and interest to individual episodes. The following examples prove that all sorts of theatrical devices can be introduced into action scenarios for dramatic effect and audience interest. They are like little subplots in the pageant story, and in many cases they deal with the introduction of artifacts, characters, or perhaps even animals.

We have already spoken of the fact that everything in a pageant is painted in broad strokes. With this in mind, it is a good idea to enlarge the picture by introducing outsized artifacts into crowd scenes. In one pageant in an episode having to do with the influence of the prophets of the Bible on the thinking of the Puritans, the Pilgrim Fathers gathered on the forestage to adopt the Mayflower Compact. At the same time, a procession of biblical prophets passed across the back of the stage in a sort of shadow, each accompanied by an attendant carrying some outsize object whose outline was familiar. There were, for instance, Tablets of the Law, seven-branched candlesticks, and the like. There was no mistaking what was being represented. And it was also very effective visually. So, though the Prophets themselves looked alike, with their long beards and white robes, it was easy to tell which prophet was which.

Wheeled vehicles are also effective props: a market wagon or two, a gentleman's coach or a one-horse shay. In the 175th anniversary celebration of the Declaration of Independence, John Hancock arrived by coach. Instead of horses, Liberty Boys pulled the coach on stage. And though Caesar Rodney was supposed to have ridden up from Delaware (in that same pageant, a real horse was used), a hostler ran down and seized the bridle so that Rodney could dismount and walk up onto the stage.

Animals are wonderful to have in pageants, but they're very chancy. They must be thoroughly, quietly, and individually rehearsed, and only gradually introduced into the scenes with actors. They are very easily distracted. To music especially, they are susceptible, and must be completely accustomed to the sound of a band or they won't behave properly on the stage. It's wise to include a street cleaner as a character in the cast!

In preparation for one pageant where we used horses, dogs, and oxen, for a week before the performance we had a noisy high school band go into the stable and march up and down, blaring marches and waltzes. The first few days the animals were panicky, but by the end of the week, a trombone player could go up to the most skittish horse and play right in his face without causing the animal to flick an ear.

In this same pageant a character was used who was very popular with audiences. This was a tall itinerant preacher riding along, seated on a small donkey, reading his prayer book. Donkeys make very good actors if you can only discover their likes and dislikes. We found out that this particular donkey was fond of pickles. We rehearsed him again and again, leading him across the stage to a spot where the assistant stage manager was waiting with a pickle. When the donkey finally realized that if he took this short walk, he would be rewarded with his favorite food, he could hardly wait to do his act. We had no trouble with him in the pageant. Indeed, we used the same character in many other pageants with donkeys that favored less exotic fare.

Dogs are very decorative, but don't use them without their masters.

In one pageant we had an organ grinder with a monkey, but this monkey was used to crowds and completely under the domination of his owner. Don't let anybody but the owner handle a monkey, for these little animals bite when they are frightened. Cats too are colorful, but they're very hard to control, even when carried by someone they know. It's best to bring your cat on stage in a basket, if you must have one.

Once we were able to use a flock of sheep with great success. This was possible because one of our actors was a small boy with a pet goat, very well trained, and since sheep always follow goats, we had no trouble there. But we never took another chance.

Mules are very hard to handle and very temperamental. In one pageant, mules were used to pull a canal boat across the stage. One of them would never move beyond a certain point on the stage until we found that the noise made by my jangling bracelets made it nervous and it wouldn't pass me. All I had to do was remove the bracelets.

In another pageant we used three mules, two brown and one white. We wanted the white mule to lead, but we soon found out that it was not a lead mule, and our esthetic ideas had to be put aside for practical reasons. We had a time figuring out which of the brown mules was the lead mule, but we finally solved that mystery and marked one of its ears with what we thought was an indelible marker. Occasionally the mark rubbed off in the stable, and we had to go through the whole rigamarole again before the mules would parade in line.

The object of recalling these stories is to show how important detail is in building up a pageant. It is with this warning in mind that the reader should go on to Part VI.

Part VI

○○○

REHEARSALS!
REHEARSALS!
REHEARSALS!

16 The Business of Rehearsing

BETWEEN THE FIRST GET-TOGETHER and the last general rehearsal (the rehearsal before the dress rehearsal and the performance), rehearsals must be called as often as possible.

PROCEDURE

Exactly how many rehearsals are necessary? There is no hard and fast answer to this question. From here on the entire production is broken down into small bits and each bit is rehearsed as often as necessary to get it really working. The amount of rehearsal that each episode, scene, or subscene needs depends to a great extent on its intricacy and the flexibility of the actors. A procession, for instance, should not need as many rehearsals as a dramatic act or a dance sequence; but taking a tip from what we have just said about detail, even a procession, if it is to be interesting, will be made up of individuals, each with his own particular character. Every one of these persons needs individual rehearsing.

For the next several weeks we begin by holding small, short rehearsals. Only the scenes which are actually to be rehearsed and the people who will work in them are called. Episode Three, for instance, is called. Epi-

sode One is called half an hour later; Interlude Two, a half or three-quar-
ters of an hour later. If you have more than one room in which to rehearse, you can have several rehearsals going at the same time, but the
important thing is that every person who shows up gets to do his part. Nobody sits around and waits. Nothing is more destructive to the morale of
amateurs than to sit around and watch other people rehearse. Call only
those for each rehearsal who will actually have something to do. If somebody is missing, have your stage managers fill in.

But above all, *don't wait for anybody*. Make it an absolute rule to start
every rehearsal *on time*.

Call frequent rehearsals. Try to get your actors in to work several
times a week so that they get the feeling that they are so busy rehearsing
they have no leisure time for anything else.

There is another reason for frequent rehearsals. They keep amateurs
from forgetting what they learned the last time.

Call rehearsals whenever you can get your actors—morning, noon, or
night. Housewives may be able to come at one time, children at another,
business people at another. Having even two or three people to work up
a small segment of a scene is worthwhile and adds something to the production. Sometimes one person may want his own rehearsal. Slide that
in too. Keep the actors busy! At first give them simple directions and add
something each time, so that they have a feeling of building up their
interpretation. Guard against a mechanical repetition of what they know
from the last time they rehearsed. The important thing is to break the
rehearsals down into small units so that each actor may feel that he is
getting the maximum amount of personal attention.

These individual rehearsals can be run by the stage managers, but the
director must arrange his schedule in such a way that he is present at
least part of the time at every single rehearsal, no matter how small.
With amateurs, I have found that it is sometimes well to actually demon-
strate how to do something, to act out parts for them. The sight of the
director, miming and acting unself-consciously—even sort of playing the
fool—may free "up-tight" actors from any embarrassment and make
them let go. At the same time, caution them against mere imitation. Remind them that what they have to give to the audience is the creation of
their own character in their own way.

Professional actors have technique and training to fall back on, but
amateurs develop their parts in an entirely different way. They bring a
sincerity and realism to their performance that takes the place of technique. But they must always be kept interested and fresh. They become
stale quickly if they lose their enthusiasm.

The stage manager must display the blown-up floor plans with their
crayon marks of each episode at every rehearsal, even the smallest. In

this way, the actors can become familiar not only with their own positions on the stage, but with the positions of the people in the overall scene in which they will eventually appear, who have not been called for this particular rehearsal.

Then when two parts of an episode are brought together for rehearsal, the sections will fit like pieces of a jigsaw puzzle. As time goes on and the individual actors become comfortable and confident in their own roles, you are ready for the next step.

Gradually the rehearsals become larger, gradually more and more people are added at each rehearsal. Episodes are filled out and combined, the narrator is brought in, the music introduced. Little by little, the entire episode can be run through without wasting time. It is unwise at these larger rehearsals to stop too often and keep a whole crowd of people standing around while you give instructions to a few. So continue to hold extra individual rehearsals, when necessary, between these larger rehearsals.

Early rehearsals should be held indoors; people are easier to manage in limited areas. But as soon as you can, as they get familiar with their parts and relax, take your cast for a visit to the site of the pageant. Take them several times so they may compare the space in which they have been rehearsing to the space in which they will play. It is difficult for amateurs to envision a big area if they have been rehearsing in a small one, even though they have been studying the floor plan designs. Seeing the place where they will eventually act helps them enlarge their gestures and their acting scope in a natural way.

Be sure to allow time at every rehearsal for sitting, standing, gesticulating, and walking exercises—the same exercises the actors learned the first time they met.

Also allow time out from the first small rehearsals for the costume committee to take measurements. The committee members need these measurements before they can go to work and make the costumes.

In this way, bit by bit, the entire show is built up.

Not only have we integrated the pageant, but we have welded the participants together into a viable whole. People acting together in a dramatic presentation seem to set up a sort of esprit de corps in their make-believe. This often carries over into real life, and can last far beyond the event itself, bringing a new dimension to the community. Race, religion, politics—all are forgotten in the joy of abstract creation. In many cases this welding of different elements is just as important as the fact that a well-advertised, well-produced pageant boosts business.

Thus we have been getting ready painlessly for the general rehearsals. Try to call these general rehearsals for the times most convenient for the majority of the actors. You'll need them!

If the pageant is to be out of doors, it's a good idea to ask the Weather Bureau to do a little research on the weather conditions for the last five years on the dates you prefer, and gamble along with the weather man. Of course, there's no way of guaranteeing good weather. Lincoln's Gettysburg Address was November 19, 1863. For the centennial the date was put forward a month because for the ten years preceding, November 19 had been stormy. To everybody's disgust, November 19, 1963 turned out to be a beautiful day. But it was too late to do anything about it. The pageant had been over for a month.

Under any circumstances, be sure to allow for a spell of bad weather. When it rains actors don't show up and traffic is uncertain.

The first general rehearsal should take place ten days to a week before the performance.

PULLING THE SHOW TOGETHER

These ten days before the performance are crucial ones. During this period everybody concerned, backstage and onstage, must be willing to give everything to the important task of getting the show together. The technical staff, the costume committee, the stage managers, the actors themselves must stand ready to devote every possible moment, good-naturedly and willingly, to these important days. Now the entire production must be rehearsed in its proper sequence from beginning to end.

There should be four such rehearsals, plus a complete dress rehearsal. The purpose of these rehearsals is to put together what has been learned in the small rehearsals, to give them pace and rhythm, to accustom the participants to the order and timing both onstage and off, so that the complete pageant can be gone through in a single evening approximately the way it will be done at the performance.

The first of these rehearsals is what professionals might call a "walk-through." The stage managers learn to bring their groups on and off stage in the proper sequence on cue with no delay. The actors run through their parts and get to know their own positions on the stage, learn their relation to the other performers, and their part in the entire pageant.

The second of these get-togethers is a costume parade. The actors dress, familiarize themselves with their props, and learn to wear and manage their clothes. The director, the designer, and the costume committee get a chance to look them over.

The third "go-around" is again a complete rehearsal. Again actors carry all their props and those whose costumes needed alterations between the dress parade and this rehearsal, or who found them difficult to manage, put them on again. This time the emphasis in the rehearsal is on the synchronization of the action with the narration, the music, and the lights (if any).

The fourth rehearsal is a repetition of the third, and here some refinements may be added and the timing stabilized.

After these preliminaries the big dress rehearsal should run smoothly.

All the old wives' tales you have heard about a bad dress rehearsal promising a good performance is just so much nonsense. Indeed in many cases the director might think it safe to invite groups like the Boy Scouts to attend the dress rehearsal as guests. Don't, however, invite the sponsors, for a dress rehearsal never has the verve of a first night. And an occasional halt might be absolutely necessary on dress rehearsal night.

FIRST GENERAL REHEARSAL

The main concern of the director and his assistants at the small rehearsals has been to keep his volunteers at fever heat in order to sustain their real enthusiasm for the project and carry it into the actual performance. It is during the general rehearsals that it is difficult to maintain this high pitch. For these rehearsals, no matter how well planned, are almost certain to be long and, of necessity, some people find themselves standing around and getting bored and discontented. There are several reasons for this. The first general rehearsal, especially, is quite a finicky job, for it is here that the different episodes are brought together and coordinated for the first time. In addition, if there are any big props, this is when they are introduced. Moreover, if we have any animals to deal with, the animals rate special attention. Animals are easily confused even if they have been well rehearsed before (and a rehearsal with an animal means doing the same thing over and over again until the pattern of his performance is well set). When they see people milling around whom they haven't seen before, and hear noises that they haven't heard, they may get jumpy. Anything is liable to happen unexpectedly at the first general rehearsal and must be dealt with promptly and patiently, not only by the director and the people involved, but by the members of the cast standing around waiting. The difficult thing is to keep the "waiters" quiet and happy. Invite a "Coke" or "Good Humor" man to be present. He'll do a land office business.

The call for this rehearsal is handled in the same manner as the small rehearsals, only this time in proper order. The actors in Episode One are called at 7:00, Interlude One at 7:45, Episode Two at 8:15, etc. As always, start on time, don't linger over details, and try to finish as the next group arrives. If you are not adamant about this, you will never finish the whole thing in one evening. Make notes or have one of your stage managers make your notes through the run-through, but unless things get helplessly tangled, *don't stop the rehearsal to give instructions.* However, before each group is dismissed, their stage manager calls a small special rehearsal the next day. At that time all the notes made at the general rehearsal are discussed and any changes necessary are made. At this first big rehearsal the *flow* of the production is reached for, so that the actors will have some idea of the *rhythm* for which you are striving, and so that the production will have some pace. If you stop too often for corrections, you interrupt this continuity.

The question of pace is an extremely subtle one, and has to do directly with the nature of pageant production. Just as words and music and big groups and little groups are the basic elements of variety in pageants, change of tempo is the icing on the cake. Nothing is more deadly dull to an audience than watching everybody walk on stage with exactly the same cadence, to hear words read in the same rhythm, to see groups move in a repetitive pattern. A pageant is a symphony; the actors are the notes, the narrators are the melodies, and the pace is the tempo. If Benjamin Franklin and a group of signers enter slowly, talking together, and Caesar Rodney suddenly rushes in on his horse, we have a good example of a change of pace. Or if a patriot Quaker lady crosses the stage defiantly while a group of workmen loiter by, you once more have this contrast. It's as simple as that and as difficult to achieve unless you know what the effect is that you are trying for.

In short, to get the actors comfortable in their relation to each other and to the whole production, to get some idea of the timing, to find out what small details need rectifying, and to set the pace—these are the objects of this run-through or first general rehearsal.

This run-through is also of great importance to the narrators. They are getting their first shot at reading the script as a continuity while the actors perform with it. And the music director should also attend closely and use this opportunity to have the score played through at least by a pianist (who will also play in the orchestra at the performance). The music director will even have a chance to study his singers and onstage musicians as they do their parts.

SECOND GENERAL REHEARSAL OR DRESS PARADE

The dress or costume parade follows closely the first general rehearsal. Preparations for this event have been going on for a long time. Naturally, every actor has tried on his costume at least once before and has had it fitted by the costume committee, and he is familiar more or less with what he is expected to wear. We have described earlier how the actors'

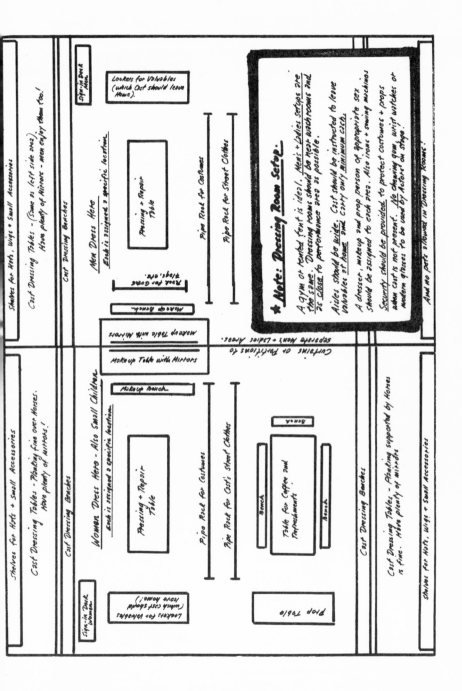

costumes have been sorted out, group by group, and how gradually their hand props and small ornaments have been placed together with their costumes. Now the actors are going to use them.

Members of the costume committee, the dressers and the stage managers have arranged a row of hangers for each group. On these hangers or in a container under them go not only the dress or suit each actor wears, but his underwear, his stockings, special ornamentation for his shoes, his hat or bonnet, and his hand props. The stage managers have made tags for these hangers bearing the name of the actor and the part he will play and a complete list of objects that belong to him. There is also a duplicate list which every character will get as he comes in to dress for the parade.

Thus, at the final performance, the actor will already be familiar with what he is supposed to wear and carry.

Once this preliminary work is done it is time for the dress parade. There should be a schedule. Actors should be called group by group so that no one is kept standing around and waiting.

As each group is costumed, the actors present themselves for inspection to the costume chairman, a fitter, the designer, and the director. They make notes of any missing object and any serious alteration. Small alterations can often be made on the spot. (Those safety pins again!) Then the actors parade up and down learning how to manage their clothes. This is especially for women who wear hoops and long dresses and trains, for the modern girl takes steps much too long for the graceful manipulation of an eighteenth-century skirt.

While the next group is dressing, the first group runs through a short rehearsal, thus getting further practice in becoming used to their clothes and hand props. People who wear gloves should be wearing them, also fans, reticules, luggage, bird cages, buckles, flowers, and above all, any documents to be carried. All of these things which have been assembled by the props committee, and which have been placed with the actors' costumes, should be used at every rehearsal from now on. It is a great advantage if the props have been brought to the small rehearsals so that the characters have become used to handling them. However, after each such rehearsal, the stage managers must be sure that the props are returned to their original places.

If for some good reason, a prop is not available till the last moment, a simulated prop should be substituted so that the characters know that they have to have them. Nothing is more destructive to a theatrical effect, for instance, than a character rushing on stage supposedly carrying, let us say, a copy of the Declaration of Independence, only to arrive without it. The fact that he has practiced his scene with some object in his hands, even if it is only a substitute, makes him know he is responsible

Individual Dressing Room Setup

Hat Box
Alfred Stern

Every Actors complete wardrobe including hand props, hats, shoes + undergarments are assembled, tagged with actor's name and hung in actor's designated Dressing Room area. Fragile items such as hats are kept in boxes. The right Corsets and full petticoats are essential for period costumes.

Individual Dressing Room Setup.

Every one is an individual and should
be assigned their own Dressing Room Area.
The right corset is important for period costumes
So are full petticoats

Alfred Stern.

for having it, and if, before he is ready for his cue, the object is missing, he will realize the omission himself and will look for it (see the discussion of the stage managers' duties in Part IV).

As the second group comes in for inspection, the first group is released. But they are not dismissed. Now is the time to take any group or individual pictures that the publicity people may wish. This is a precaution against photographers wandering around backstage the night of the performance and getting underfoot. After the pictures are taken, the group is still not dismissed until they have gone to the place where they dressed and placed their costumes on the proper hangers and their small objects in the proper containers. Make them wait until the dressers have checked the lists to see that everything is there. This is the only way to prevent money from being wasted on lost articles. Actors have a way of not replacing belts, muskets, stocks, petticoats, fichus—things that they will need for the next rehearsal. Since many of these things have to be rented, and are very costly to replace (and all small things are finicky), a check must be made of them each time after they are used. Often, when something is missing after a rehearsal, and a time-consuming fruitless search has been made, the actor arrives at the next rehearsal bringing the object with him.

So it's well for the dressers to make a telephone call to an actor who may perhaps have walked off with something carelessly, or purposely to show it to the folks at home.

In case one person plays more than one character, his costumes should be hung together instead of in his group, and a dresser should stand ready to help him make the change. The casting chairman must be sure that each actor in such a case is cast in scenes far enough apart to allow him time between his appearances to get into his second costume.

It is at the dress parade the actors learn from the director or the designer to wear and manage any part of their costume that needs management—a hoop skirt, a train, a banner, a piece of luggage, a sign. Above all, as we said before, each actor must practice with his hand props. If the actual object itself is not available, he must be given something to carry in its place: an umbrella instead of a cane, a woman's pocketbook instead of a carpetbag, a blank piece of paper in place of a document, so he gets used to holding something and knows that he can't do his job without it. But no matter what he uses in the rehearsal, he must hand it back to his dresser or his stage manager before he leaves. We cannot say too often that every actor must learn not to go on stage without his props and not to leave the rehearsal carrying them away with him.

As the clothes are hung up one by one, a fitter, stage manager, or dresser makes a list of alterations which are needed, and pins it to the costume to be altered. This is so that the costume committee can know what there is to be done in each case. If the alteration is a serious one, an engagement should be made with the actor to come in for a fitting. These fittings should, if possible, be at the actor's convenience, at a businessman's lunch hour or on the way home from school for a child, and they should be prompt and short.

Then and only then are the actors dismissed.

For the dress parade every actor must be made up and wear his wig, headdress, or hat. Stocks, neckties, and fichus should be tied and adjusted properly.

In order to make it possible for the actors who were kept late at the first general rehearsal to come early this time, it would be perfectly practical to do the whole dress parade backwards, calling the last group first, and the first group last. This is sometimes a good gimmick and doesn't affect the overall purpose of the dress parade, which is to check all costumes.

Now the stage managers read to the actors a list of things to do and not to do on the night of the performance. These include warnings against bringing money or pocketbooks which must be left where they dress, what kind of shoes to wear, what kind of jewelry they are permitted, and also a caution against chewing gum.

THIRD GENERAL REHEARSAL

Now is the time to rehearse the finale, in which everybody takes part. The backstage people, stage managers, and so forth are used to being called and staying for the entire session. But this rehearsal is the first at which everyone is called at the same hour. Unless properly and firmly conducted, but with absolute cool, it can be a fearsome ordeal, for indeed it is tedious. This is the moment of "brinkmanship," when confusion and a letdown feeling can be averted only by creating a spirit of anticipation and reality that will, hopefully, be dynamically carried into the performance. Musicians, dressers, costume committee, and almost the entire cast will have to stay till the bitter end.

Although this is not a dress rehearsal, anyone who has had trouble with any detail of his costume should be encouraged to dress so he can have some more practice in wearing it naturally and with style. Also this is another opportunity to try out any character makeup. Any costume that needs altering and has been adjusted since the dress parade must be worn. But, dressed or not, every single participant must carry and *use* his hand prop, whether it is a parasol, a pair of gloves, a reticule, a book, a document, a torch, and especially any large artifact that is brought on stage in place of scenery.

This is the first rehearsal at which the entire orchestra performs. Before this the actors have been rehearsing with a piano, or at most, with a piano and one or two instruments. But this time the full orchestra will play. It is at this rehearsal that music, narration, action, and lights are synchronized, sometimes a very delicate operation for the musicians. The narrators and actors have had rehearsals and presumably know how to go through their parts smoothly, and any stops or repeats this time should be at the request of the music director.

Before the cast assembles, the music director should have a run-through of the music with his orchestra. He must call his people early so that when your cast arrives, there are no waits.

By now everybody is used to showing up on time, a full cast is present, and without delay the finale is set up. The finale should be simple. Everybody is brought on stage and since there is no curtain, leaves the stage in a sort of processional. The description of the pageant celebrating the 175th anniversary of the signing of the Declaration of Independence in Part III gives details of one such finale.

Another way of handling the finale is to have the cast assemble on the stage. Then bring the large artifacts downstage and mass them together. Then the cast leaves the stage behind the improvised curtain. When the artifact bearers march off in formation, the stage is empty. For instance, costumed bearers could come downstage carrying an enormous facsimile of the Declaration of Independence. This would form a sort of curtain behind which the cast could disperse.

At the first Chicago Railroad Fair, a full-sized locomotive moved slowly across the forestage from left to right. After the locomotive had passed, the stage was entirely empty.

After the finale is set and quickly rehearsed, go back to Episode One and play the entire pageant through, including the finale, as you are going to do it the night of the performance.

This time the entire rehearsal should be run by the production stage manager and his assistants. The director should say nothing unless things get hopelessly snarled, but again he should make notes. In this way the cast gets used to taking its instructions from the stage managers, as they will do at the actual performance.

Of course, all choruses, singers, bands or dance groups, who have been rehearsed separately, take part in this rehearsal, and all technicians who have had their own practice sessions will also take part. This is not only a music rehearsal, but it is a light rehearsal as well, and a scenery rehearsal, and rehearsal of the sound system, and of any of the multimedia that may be used. The actors themselves get the least attention. They already know their positions and what is required of them, and they must be ready to do their parts and obey their stage managers. This is no time for temperament.

At this rehearsal the technicians may find it necessary to fix something on stage while action is going on. Nothing seems to disturb amateurs more than extraneous workers walking around them while they are trying to do their parts. It is this that differentiates amateurs from professionals.

In a big ANTA benefit some years ago, I saw Dame Judith Anderson rehearse a scene from *Medea* at the same moment at which a dance team was running through their routine stage right. Carpenters and lighting men were swarming all over the place. At the edge of the stage apron Bert Lahr was crouched down, running through his cues with the orchestra.

But it takes real professionals to concentrate on their own work in the midst of such chaos. It would be unreasonable to expect expertise like this from any amateur. The best one can hope for is cheerful cooperation during this trying rehearsal time. These big rehearsals are a real exercise in self-control for everybody, the people in charge as well as the actors. Any relaxation of good humor can act as a fuse to turn the entire rehearsal into a shambles.

Nevertheless, sometimes a well-planned, sudden, short, purposeful explosion by the director can clear the atmosphere and result in stunned acquiescent calm. Now if he finds a temper tantrum necessary, the director has to be willing to bear the resultant criticism that is almost sure to come—but not until after the rehearsal is over.

After the actors have finished on the stage and hung away their clothes and been dismissed, there is still work for the costume committee. Perhaps they would prefer to do it the next day. But the stage managers and the director, the designer, and the music director must meet, no matter how late the hour. At this meeting they will discuss the notes that have been made during the rehearsal and decide how and when any changes must be made. Perhaps the music director will want to talk with his musicians then and there (extra music rehearsals are costly). On the other hand, if the stage managers think it necessary, they can call individual rehearsals for the next day, and certainly the designer and his committees can use that time for alterations and adjustments.

Leave a day for these chores before calling the next general rehearsal.

FOURTH GENERAL REHEARSAL

If everything has gone according to schedule, this rehearsal is an extra

bonus. If, however, you have been rained out or something has pre-
vented you from holding the third general rehearsal, conduct this in the
same way.

If it is a bonus rehearsal, conduct it as calmly, as routinely, as realistic-
ally as possible. Under these circumstances it should take very little
longer than the performance itself.

Once more start with the finale, and then go through the entire pageant. If you can keep your actors in the right mood, get the cast to stay
for the whole rehearsal so that you can once more run through the finale
in its proper place. On the other hand, if you get a sensation of restless-
ness, dismiss each episode as you rehearse it. Save your ammunition for
the dress rehearsal.

It is taken for granted that in between rehearsal three and rehearsal
four, the time has been used to make any changes with individual actors,
musicians, narrators, and technicians in small special rehearsals. *Don't
stop this time to make any corrections.* Start exactly on time and *go
through the whole thing as though it were a performance. Don't interrupt the mood, the pace, and the rhythm unless something is terribly
wrong.* If you absolutely have to stop, explain to everybody exactly what
has happened. These rules can't be repeated too often.

17 Dress
Rehearsal

NINE TIMES OUT OF TEN this is the real test. We are down at last
to what might be called the "nitty gritty." It's now or never.

THE PROBLEM

There is a tradition in the theater that a bad dress rehearsal means a
good performance. To me, this is nonsense. The real problem here is to
impress on everybody the necessity for patience and fortitude, for there
is really nothing in the world more boring than a dress rehearsal. This
time the people in the first episode get dressed, and while they are running through their rehearsal, the people in the next episode get dressed

and made up, and so on to the end. There must be no pause or waiting between episodes. Each episode *must* be ready to come on *exactly* on cue, and so on and so on. Everybody, with no exception, must stay straight through the evening, so that they can participate in the finale.

AFTER THE FINALE

Nor is the ordeal over with the finale. The actors, the costume committee, and the stage managers again have to stay after the finale to put away their costumes in the already described manner so that nothing goes wrong on the night of the performance. And even after the actors have left, the stage managers and the costume people have to stay and check, to see that everything is in order for the performance. Sometimes it's possible to put off this checking until the next morning, if the stage managers and costume committee are free to come then. For there will inevitably be some things misplaced and some minor alterations to be made. Altogether, this is an ordeal and there is no use pretending that it isn't. Its success is entirely dependent on the enthusiasm and good will that is engendered during the preparation period. Even if things go smoothly, don't expect to get a thrilling dress rehearsal. Let the actors save their best energies for the performance. They should go away from the dress rehearsal determined to do even better on the big evening.

DRESS REHEARSAL AUDIENCE

When the general rehearsals have gone very well, you may be willing to arrange for a special invited audience to see the dress rehearsal. This, only in case you are going to charge for admission to the performance. The invited audience must consist of Boy or Girl Scouts or public school children and such. Actually, it is better if you don't do this, for if the dress rehearsal isn't up to standard, you'll get bad word-of-mouth publicity.. If, on the other hand, the executives want to come, the chances are they will go away discouraged. Be sure that they understand that they're looking at a rehearsal and not a performance. They should not judge the final product by what they see, and they certainly must not spread the word of their discouragement.

It is impossible to put "pace"—that elusive extra ingredient—into a dress rehearsal. That comes only with the excitement of the first night.

The dress rehearsal is no way to judge the quality of a production. It's a long, hard pull. It's the darkness before the dawn. But if the project has been well organized, if the rehearsals have been well run, there is every reason to believe that everything is ready and all signals are set for go!

18 You're On!

Here are a few simple requests which will help insure the success of the performance (Date & Time).

1. Don't bring valuables or large sums of money at any time when costume changes are made.

2. All ladies wear regular street makeup.

3. All ladies wear white or black gloves.

4. All ladies wear simple, comfortable pump type shoes. No open toes. All gentlemen wear black shoes or black boots.

5. All gentlemen who play dignitaries wear white gloves. Bring them if you have a pair.

6. Don't wear wrist watches. Please, please - no chewing gum!

7. Steel rim or rimless glasses may be worn if essential. No shell rim glasses please.

8. In the event any ladies are without gloves, they should <u>not</u> wear nail polish (unless they are playing trollops).

9. Gentlemen should <u>not</u> have haircuts prior to the performance, please.

10. All ladies will dress at (designated ladies dressing room area).

11. All gentlemen will dress at (designated men's dressing room area).

12. All children under 10 will dress in ladies dressing room area. Boys 10 and older will dress in gentlemen's dressing room area. Girls 10 and older will dress in ladies dressing room area.

13. Entire cast will sign in and when dressed are requested not to leave assigned dressing areas until they take their places for the production. Do not go anyplace where you will be seen by the audience prior to making your stage entrance. No backstage visitors or pets, please.

14. In order that the presentation may begin on time, dressing room areas will be open and functioning 3 hours before curtain time. Come as early as possible. Bring a book, cards, crossword puzzles, etc., to amuse yourself.

15. Requests for information about our production indicates huge attendance. Our success depends on you and your cooperation in all phases.

<u>EVERY SINGLE INDIVIDUAL IS EQUALLY IMPORTANT</u>

Many thanks. Good Luck to all of us, and may we make this a memorable occasion.

(Signed) *B. Davis*

Production Stage Manager.

Production Stage Manager's Memo to all Members of the Cast

19 After
the Ball

AFTER THE SHOW everybody seems to want to get together and gossip about the great event. This is a good time, while the enthusiasm is still high, to recruit volunteers to help the costume committee in what is a far from glamorous chore.

When the last performance is over, just as after dress rehearsal, the production stage manager, his assistants, the dressers, and the members of the costume committee have to be on hand to see that every actor puts his clothes and his props in their proper place. However, that's not all. Within the next twenty-four hours all costumes and artifacts must be double-checked and the chairman must be notified in writing if anything is missing. And they're not finished yet. They still have to play out what is probably one of the most important and least romantic episodes in any show. They have to pack.

It's easy to see from this why the names of all backstage people should be duly noted on the program and that they must be rewarded with compliments and publicity, and why it is a good idea to let them have their own costumes so that they can appear in the finale.

If this last get-together can be turned into a sort of reunion-kaffee-klatch, complete perhaps with coffee and cake, the tedious job of packing can be made into a party.

People who have met regularly, especially to make costumes, seem to become very close, and most unlikely friendships develop. I recall that in several instances romances have resulted between workers. There's something about being together on a project that makes for good human relationships. It is another intangible "plus" for an anniversary celebration, and another reason for producing a Bicentennial pageant.

Part VII

○○

OTHER
DRAMATIC FORMS

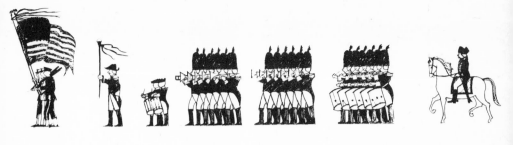

20 Parades

PERHAPS YOUR STEERING COMMITTEE has decided to hold a parade.

A parade, to be successful, must be organized in the same manner as a show. In other words, you have your steering committee, your group of professionals, your scenario, your costumes, your narrator, your music, your participants and your stage manager. But no rehearsals with the cast are necessary. There are, however, special features of a parade which must be dealt with—floats, participants, and logistics.

Let us consider the logistics first. The problem in a parade is to have it continuous. This means that it is necessary to work out a plan in which the different units "fall in" at the beginning at a specified time and place, and, at the end, "fall out" and return to their starting place in an orderly manner. Otherwise, there will be gaps in your march and chaos at your fall-out point. Also, under the heading "logistics" is the proper placing of bands.

The simplest way to make sure that your units will "fall in" in correct sequence, is to have the groups assemble by sections at selected off-parade route spots at a stated time, perhaps in buses, already costumed and aware of the scene which they represent. Each group has its own marshal and assistants. Each marshal lines up the members of his group in proper order and marches them to a place to wait, usually a side street *off* the parade route. The marshals can be thought of as stage managers and the groups are like actors, waiting in the wings for their cue. On cue, each group joins the line of march, falling in, in proper sequence and with proper cadence.

This cadence is set up by the bands, choruses, or special musicians, who also march in the parade, and who have assembled from their off-stage positions and fall in on their own cues.

Their music must be selected with an understanding of what kind of group they are to lead. In order to keep the marchers properly spaced, the rhythms of different musical elements must not be too divergent. (By musical elements, we mean a band, a chorus, a special group of fifers and drummers, a German band or a group of trumpeters, and so on.) Each band should have a set music program. Music makers must be spaced carefully. They must not be so close together that their music overlaps, but should be close enough to avoid silences and keep the parade lively. For this reason, the music makers must not only be spaced carefully but, throughout the march, they must be scheduled to play and stop, according to plan. If, as we hope, there will be narrators—

people describing over a loudspeaker what contingent is passing at that moment—there should be *no* playing where the narrators are stationed.

The music units assemble in the same offstage spot as the actors. They get their cue first and strike up in the side street (or wings) half a minute or so before actually joining the march. In this way, the marchers (or actors) behind them know the pace at which they must walk in the parade.

As in a show, the most tedious part of a parade comes at the end when the fun is over. At the end of the line of march there should be a parking space provided, so that the floats and large props can be left there. The characters in each group, still in formation and carrying their hand props, return to their original starting place, there to be loaded into the buses and dismissed as a group by their marshals. Under no circumstances, should the group be allowed to disintegrate at the terminal point of the parade, no matter how they are costumed. People are people, and are almost sure to run back to take a look at what is following them. This will cause a traffic jam, and will be felt all the way along the line of march.

So much for logistics.

Now let us consider the floats. A parade, like any spectacle, should have a theme. To have a really successful parade, this theme should be developed through a scenario. Each marching group and float should represent a different episode or scene in the scenario. Certainly, any parade for the celebration of the Declaration of Independence must have such a scenario. Otherwise, a glut will arrive of groups representing signers or Liberty Boys, and we will have dozens of George Washingtons and Marquis de Lafayettes, and nothing else. I remember seeing a Civil War parade in which there were five Robert E. Lees on Traveler, and even more J.E.B. Stuarts. After the third of the heroes passed, the spectators on the sidewalks laughed, hooted and booed.

On the other hand, the great parade to celebrate the 350th anniversary

of the founding of the City of Detroit had a strict scenario, and the participants vied with one another in carrying out, through the use of floats and marchers, the story of the history of the city.

Having a scenario means that there will be a standard which the groups must meet. This standard must be especially stringent for the floats. Otherwise, Hose Company No. 62, for instance, will have a well-made, well-designed float, and Grammar School No. 4 will come with some rickety contraption made of cardboard. In order to avoid this inevitable contrast, the steering committee might very well collect a sum of money and allocate it for floats.

An added esthetic touch is for the steering committee to have a designer provide the groups with plans for their individual floats so that at least the beds of the floats will be harmonious. Don't, under any circumstances, let anybody do any advertising on the floats. Also, do not make any group feel that it must have a float. In the case of the school children, for instance, some period vehicles might do very well—for instance, an old-time farm wagon, a teacher in a gig. And of course there's always John Hancock with his coach and his Liberty Boys to fill in.

Be sure, however, not to have rubber tires on John Hancock's coach. There are almost always old wheels and carriage frames to be found moldering away in barns that have become garages. These can generally be put in condition by local carpenters, or maybe you'll be lucky enough to find a blacksmith to do it. A false top can be made of cardboard or plywood. Things of this sort make beautiful artifacts for the parade and are a welcome change from floats.

Like a pageant, the most tedious part of a parade comes at the end, when the fun is over. Definite plans must be made to park the floats and the artifacts and get each group back to its starting place so that it can be dismissed by the marshals. Since each group is probably responsible for its own costumes, that trying chore can be left to each of them to work out themselves. However, if at all possible, the steering committee should try to set up some standard, especially in a small parade.

21 Dedications

THERE ARE ALL SORTS OF THINGS that can be dedicated or rededicated. We have already spoken about tree plantings. There is also the idea of the unveiling of a plaque on a historic site. And, of course, the opening of old houses for public inspection.

In the first two cases a very simple pageant can accompany the ceremony. Try to integrate any speeches to be made into the pageant and have some sort of plan for the speechmaking. This is a wonderful opportunity for the chairman of the steering committee to exercise his tact. Nothing is more boring for an audience than to stand around while some local V.I.P. or even some Washington luminary drones on and on. Select a theme for your production and don't hesitate to ask the speakers to conform to this theme, and tell them how long they are to speak. If you want them to speak fifteen minutes, ask them for ten, for no speaker, except those on television and radio has ever been known to confine himself within the time limit set.

An example of a very successful plaque unveiling occurred on the occasion of the Bicentennial of Columbia University, when a plaque was placed on the United States Steel Company's skyscraper in downtown New York at the site of the first class of Columbia (then King's) College. The opening address was made by the dean of the university, costumed as the first president of the college. A short dramatic presentation followed, in which he took part, representing the first class assembly. The narrator was Bennett Cerf, an alumnus. The dramatization ended just as the clock in the tower of Trinity Church nearby (in the rectory of which the first class met) struck twelve. At the last stroke, the president of the United States Steel Company, in modern clothes, stepped out, made a short speech dealing with the part the university has played in the history of New York, and unveiled the plaque. The actors marched into the building and the dedication was over. The whole thing took less than an hour. The ceremony was mercifully brief because all traffic had been stopped on Broadway and Rector Street at the lunch hour on a busy week day. But its very brevity sent the audience away in good humor.

22 Restorations and
Historic Houses

IT IS MORE THAN LIKELY that the Revolutionary Bicentennial years will trigger an explosion of restorations of historic sites and especially historic houses. The President's National Commission is putting special emphasis on this kind of activity, hoping that through the stimulus of the Bicentennial many worthwhile sites and buildings will be preserved that might otherwise be condemned to the bulldozer.

There are already some spots where good jobs of restoration have been done: Williamsburg, Virginia; Natchez, Mississippi; and Old Salem, North Carolina, to name a few. In most of these places certain days are set aside for tours, and the tours often are conducted by local guides dressed in costumes of the period and well briefed in the history of the place.

In some places slightly more elaborate programs are presented, such as concerts of music of the period performed on correct instruments by costumed musicians. In Williamsburg, for instance, there are concerts of chamber music in the Governor's Palace, and male carousers in the tavern. In Old Salem they use wind instruments, many of which are antiques and have been handed down from father to son—and to daughter.

A pattern like this could easily be followed in almost any restoration. It would be possible to elaborate on this pattern. Groups could present appropriate dances. Or, if a court house or public building were to be restored, there might be a dramatized meeting of the citizens, a town hall meeting, a meeting of the legislators, and the like. The subject to be discussed at such a meeting might be the town fathers' decision to accept or reject the Declaration, or some special point in the Declaration like its assertion that all men are created equal, which leads inevitably to a broadening of voting and other civil rights. If the building continued to be used after the Revolutionary period, a small, short dramatization could include later discussions of the same subject, increasing its relevancy.

If the building itself has been destroyed, it might be well to create some kind of small theatrical episode on the site, much in the spirit of the 200th anniversary celebration of Columbia College, described above under Dedications.

For all of these occasions, however, be sure to organize well, hold enough rehearsals so that it will go smoothly, and, above all, make sure that the audience is comfortable, well looked after, and if the event lasts more than ten or fifteen minutes, that the onlookers can sit down.

Once again, this type of anniversary commemoration seems to engender speechmaking. Be sure that the speeches are short, appropriate to the dramatization, and to the point. And that there are not many. Three of about eight minutes is about all that any audience can tolerate and absorb. And it is well to have at least one master of ceremonies or, preferably, narrators in costume to speak over an amplifying system so that everybody knows what's going on.

23 Vignettes

VIGNETTES ARE SMALL DRAMATIZATIONS of special events and are a splendid device when the audience must travel to more than one place. In George Washington's brother's home, splendidly restored in Fredericksburg, Virginia, an unforgettable device of this kind was set up under the guidance of Bob Porterfield, the director of Virginia's Barter Theatre, a state enterprise. As tourists were led from room to room, they saw small re-enactments of home life in each room. In the nursery, for instance, Madam Washington was reading to her grandchildren. At one point she laid down the book and gave the children a short and graphic account of an activity of General Washington. The whole thing was over in a few minutes, and the tourists were guided to the next room. This was a bedroom. On the bed lay General Washington, stretched in full regalia with his muddy boots resting on the white counterpane. A small servitor was wielding a long-handled peacock fan over the recumbent general. The costumed guide explained that General Washington had just come from a nearby battlefield, and told a little bit about the battle. Then there was silence. General Washington, still asleep, turned over on the bed. The small fan wielder ran around the bed and took up his position at the other side. He'd hardly started when General Washington turned to the other side, and the little boy once more ran around. When General Washington changed his position for the third time, the boy stopped struggling.

"General Washington," he said, "if you keep on turning from side to side, I just can't shoo the flies off you."

The guide immediately closed the door and led his group to the next room.

These were charming and human scenes and made a great impression.

On the Gettysburg battlefield, where a larger area was covered, the audience was bussed from one place to another. There was a small vignette on the porch of Meade's headquarters, where the decision to remain on Cemetery Ridge was made by Meade and his generals; at Spangler's Spring Union and Confederate soldiers fraternized; at Lee's headquarters Lee revealed the Pickett's charge strategy to General Longstreet. Other vignettes were presented at Devil's Den, the High Water Mark, and the Peach Orchard.

As each vignette came to a close, one busload left and another drove up and the scene was repeated. The schedule of this took considerable planning and it meant that the actors had to repeat the scene three or four times each day of the commemoration. The vignettes themselves, however, were extremely simple, and within the capabilities of well-rehearsed amateurs. In this sequence the narrator or M.C. rode in the bus and elaborated on each scene or prepared the audience for the next as the bus drove from spot to spot.

Vignettes of this type are not as difficult to produce as an integrated pageant. For though each vignette must have its own pace, the director is spared the agonies of putting the show together and synchronizing its many elements.

24 Happenings

AT THIS WRITING events called "happenings" are much in vogue. The impression that the promoters of such things wish to give is that a happening just happens. This is far from fact. Happenings, to be successful, must be extremely well planned.

Suppose, for instance, you announce that people are invited to record graphically their impressions of the signing of the Declaration. First, a time must be announced and a time limit set; then a place must be selected, and something to paint or draw on must be put up. The length and height of the "canvas" must be determined by the space available, the participants, number of people expected, and the length of their arms (children need a different space from grown people). Then crayons, pencils, colors, water, and so on must be provided, enough so that nobody is disappointed. The most difficult part of this kind of happening is to get the performers to stop when the time is up; so we once more have marshals or police or stage managers, or whatever you want to call them, to see that the plan is carried out, and a steering committee to collect the money for the materials. The thing that distinguishes a happening from any other kind of production is that the actors are free to do their own thing. But even so, they must stay within whatever physical limits it has been necessary to set. If, instead of an art happening, the event were to be announced as a dramatic happening, in place of canvas and colors those in charge whould have to provide a stage or acting area and a strict time limit for each presentation. Also, it might be well to guard against too much repetition. Perhaps the participants would be required in advance to indicate what characters they intend to use in their improvisation, if they intend to employ special characters. Otherwise, the entire period might be occupied by repetitions of the signing of the Declaration of Independence, with half a dozen Benjamin Franklins and an equal number of John Adamses or Thomas Jeffersons. However, this would not be too serious, for a happening is primarily for the enjoyment of the participants. The audience has only secondary rights, and if they're bored they can always leave. Remember, since a dramatic happening involves many individuals and much more action than an art happening, a good number of stage managers is a prime requirement, and they must be people with a lot of patience.

But no matter when or where or what form these celebrations take, in order to be successful they must be well organized.

25 E Pluribus
Unum

THERE IS SOMETHING rather exciting about the idea of a nation of almost 200,000,000 people examining their heritage, looking thoughtfully into its future, and exploding simultaneously in a celebration of "Brother Jonathan's Birthday."

It is for these people that this little handbook was written.

Part VIII

○○○○○○○○○○○○○○○○○○○○○○○○○○○○○○○○○○○○○○○

SOURCES AND
RESOURCES

HISTORICAL BACKGROUND*

For a good overall entertaining look at American history, the following books are recommended:

The Oxford History of the American People, Samuel Eliot Morison (Oxford University Press)

Rise of American Civilization and *A Basic History of the United States* (short), both by Charles and Mary Beard (Macmillan)

Main Currents in American Thought, Vernon L. Parrington (Harcourt)

All these are fairly easy reading, are full of prejudice, and hence stimulate the imagination.

Other books, also easy to read, and containing details of the everyday life of the Revolutionary period, in addition to listing historical events, are:

The Birth of the Nation, Arthur Schlesinger, Sr. (Putnam's)

March of Democracy, Vol. I, James Truslow Adams (Scribner's)

Secret History of the American Revolution, Carl Van Doren (Viking)

---

*This section has been prepared with the assistance of Dr. Alice K. Harris, Assistant Professor of American History at Hofstra College, Hempstead, L.I., N.Y.

All these books have been fought over and discussed by historians, and are lively reading.

Less lively, but full of salty anecdotes, is *The Education of Henry Adams,* which is now available in paperback.

Dr. Alice Harris teaches American history at Hofstra University, Long Island, with an eye to making it relevant. She has made an additional list of paperbacks. She recommends *The Birth of the Republic; 1763-1789,* Edmund Morgan (University of California, 1956). Morgan views the period as one in which Americans were searching for the principles on which they founded their freedom.

The American Revolution: A Short History, Richard B. Morris, and *The Coming of the Revolution,* Lawrence Gipson (Verti Harper, 1954) treat of the Revolution as the result of Britain's failure to give self-government to mature colonies; the first of these from the American viewpoint, the second, from the British.

Origin of the American Revolution, John C. Miller (Verti Harper, 1943) and *Triumph of Freedom* (Verti Harper, 1948) together provide a treatment of the origins and creation of the Declaration as a product of American ingenuity, while *The American Revolution: 1775-1783,* Richard Alden (American Nation Series, Harper, 1954) justifies the conduct of the patriots in carrying out the intent of the Declaration.

Seed Time of the Republic (1953), Clinton Rossiter, and *Seeds of Liberty,* Max Saville, cover the ferment of ideas which led up to the Revolution, the latter with emphasis on the Colonists as self-conscious seekers of liberty.

Many of the books on this list by Dr. Harris deal directly with specialized material, such as may have been chosen as the theme or the particular subject of our pageant.

For a very detailed free bibliography of books about the Revolutionary period, write to:

> National Bicentennial Production Service, Inc.,
> Melville Bernstein, Director,
> 15 East 48th Street, New York, N.Y. 10017

The literature available is divided into separate headings such as: "General Perspectives," "Causes and Effects," "Philosophy and Diplomacy," "The Action," "War at Sea," "The Leaders," "British Sources," "Literature and Art," and even "Fiction." Under "Other Valuable Sources," there are the names of the best state, county, and local societies and publications.

An excellent picture book with interesting text is *Ships and Seamen of the American Revolution,* Jack Coggins (Stackpole, 1969).

Some of the most stimulating books about the Revolution have been written for juveniles and young adults. Chief among these are in Random House's Landmark Series.

Trumpet of Prophecy, John Anthony Scott (Alfred Knopf, 1969) is a very "new history of the Revolution, told principally in the words of the participants." This book has some very interesting reproductions of contemporary pictures and cartoons which would be useful to the costume designer, and, indeed, because of their liveliness, might stimulate the director as well.

A Picture Book of Revolutionary War Heroes, Leonard Everett Fisher (a Giniger-Stackpole book, 1970) contains thumbnail sketches of characters and episodes that might well be dramatized. The costume details in all the illustrations, showing, for instance, different kinds of stocks and different ways of wearing belts and headgear, are very helpful and exceedingly diverse.

All the books mentioned are readily available. Many of them are probably already in the libraries of even the smallest community, and the books for young people are almost sure to be found in the school libraries as supplementary reading in American history.

Never forget that pinpointing incidents and people from your own part of the country is the key to a successful popular production. You may get some idea of the great variety of things that can be dramatized by reading the brochure recently put out by the Publishing and Library Service of the *New York Times.* In it are listed books written by "little people" who took part in the Revolution, ranging from the *Journal* of the President of the Continental Congress, the *Observations of a Loyalist Girl in Her 20's,* the *Letters* of the German baroness who rode in her coach from Quebec to Ticonderoga along with the British Army, the *Memoirs* of the head of Washington's Secret Service, to the *Adventures* of a private who escaped from a prison ship in the harbor of New York, by swimming. Write for this brochure to:

Eyewitness Accounts of the American Revolution, Arno Press, 330 Madison Avenue, New York, N.Y. 10017.

There may have been somebody in your own area who had some minor but dramatic experiences. Look him up. You may be able to find him in the more than 50-volume reference that has gone through many editions and is certainly in any good college library where history is taught. The title is *Biography of American History.*

Soak up all the information you can. This will give you a feeling for the overall intent and background of the Revolutionary period and its subsequent impact on our living today. By reading at least some of the books that have been mentioned, by haunting your local library, consulting your local historical societies and your local history fans, you can convert your pageant from a cold, generalized undertaking to a thrilling, dramatic, *living* experience.

PROFESSIONAL HELP

The type of professional—director, designer, and so forth—who is "pageant-oriented," has already been described. The question is, where do we find them?

Several universities have drama departments from which very distinguished directors have come. Chief among them are the following:

Carnegie Institute of Technology, Pittsburgh, Pa.
Northwestern University, Evanston, Ill.
The University of North Carolina, Chapel Hill, N.C.

At North Carolina, Paul Green has trained directors of many of the outstanding pageants that are taking place throughout the country, and is continuing to do so. Kennett Hunter from the same university, an active pageant director, probably has people on his list who have assisted him in his many enterprises, and whom he may be able to recommend.

Brandeis University and Boston University, Boston, Massachusetts, both have excellent and extremely modern theater departments, and a good pageantry record.

The Little Theatre and Karamu House, both in Cleveland, Ohio, are good sources of professional help.

There are outstanding groups in Portland, Oregon; Santa Fe, New Mexico; and Seattle, Washington.

ANTA has had long experience with communities and community theaters, almost every place in the United States. To make inquiries, write to:

Jean Dalrymple, c/o ANTA, ANTA Theatre,
245 West 52nd Street, New York, N.Y. 10019.

The author of this book has the names of some professionals who have worked with her on pageants. Address her c/o Stackpole Books, Cameron and Kelker Streets, Harrisburg, Pa. 17105.

Community councils of the arts have been set up in many states. There may be one in your locality. Use it.

The St. Louis Municipal Opera imports professionals every summer for their season. They may be a source of help.

The President's Commission on the Bicentennial of the American Revolution is now being organized and should be an excellent source of all kinds of information. Write to:

The Executive Director
American Revolution Bicentennial Commission
736 Jackson Place, N.W.
Washington, D.C. 20276

There are many commercial organizations who will offer to take over everything from money-raising to curtain-raising, but since this is a do-it-yourself book, they are not listed.

The real worth to a community of any Bicentennial presentation is in keeping it as localized and as relevant to the community as possible. Be sure that any professional you engage for any aspect of work understands this ideal thoroughly.

MUSIC*

Both information on the music of the Revolutionary period and the music itself are readily available. The music includes both songs and instrumental compositions.

BOOKS AND SONG BOOKS

Though published in 1948, Dr. Sigmund Spaeth's *A History of Popular Music in America* (Random House), is still the best guide to the music (with titles) of the Revolutionary period. The introduction and the first chapters list dozens of titles of the music that was composed, played, and sung during those years, with trenchant descriptions of how they were used. This book is to be found in almost any library. Use this history to authenticate any selection you may make.

Now having your background, you can examine the books which contain the actual music. Among these are:

Music in the New Found Land, Wilfred Mellers (Alfred Knopf, New York)
Music and Musicians in Early America, Irving Lowens (Norton)
America's Music, Gilbert Chase (McGraw-Hill)
Music of George Washington's Time, J. T. Howard (Washington Commission)
The New Green Mountain Songster (Yale University Press)

---

*This section was prepared with the help of Harold L. Peterson, Chief Curator of the National Park Service, and Ann Ronell, co-composer and lyricist of film scores: *Story of G.I. Joe, One Touch of Venus, Main Street to Broadway;* of the popular songs "Rain on the Roof," "Linda," and "Who's Afraid of the Big Bad Wolf"; and adapter of the Metropolitan Opera's production of *Martha.*

American Sea Songs and Chanteys, Frank Shay, Ed. (Norton)
Our Familiar Songs, Helen Kendrick Johnson (Henry Holt & Co.,1881)
National Anthems, Paul Nettl (Storm Publishing, New York)
A Williamsburg Songbook (selected and set for voices and keyboard),
   John Edmunds (Colonial Williamsburg, Va. 23185)
Songs and Music of the Redcoats, Lewis Weinstock (Stackpole, Har-
   risburg, Pa.)
Songs Under the Liberty Bell, Art Shrader (Old Sturbridge, Mass.)
Trumpet of a Prophecy (arranged for voice and guitar), Scott (Knopf)

There is a list of books containing songs of the Revolutionary period,
compiled by Moses Asch, for Folkway Records and Services, New York.

FANFARES AND SCORES

For instrumental military music and more elaborate orchestral scores,
consult the following:

Music for Fifes and Drums, The Company of Fifers and Drummers,
   c/o David Beddie, 2049 34th St., S.E., Washington, D.C.
Orchestra Score by Aaron Copeland (Boosey & Hawkes, New York,
   N.Y.)
Orchestra Score, Jeanne Behrend (Theodore Presser, Philadelphia)
Fanfares for Trumpets and Trombones, Gail Kubik (Leeds Music
   Corp., New York, N.Y.)

These last three are original compositions, embodying traditional music.

TAPES AND RECORDS

Much music of the Revolutionary era has been recorded. Among the
most valuable selections of such recorded music are the following:

Horns Only, Louis Applebaum, CBC, Totonto, Canada
Horns Only, Music Library (Shakespeare Festival, Stratford, Conn.)
Ballads of the Revolution, Folkways Album FP 48-2, FP 5001 (Folk-
   ways Records and Services, New York, N.Y.)

The songs in the last album are sung by Wallace House, with guitar accompaniment, and are particularly interesting because many of the
songs memorialize special events, like "The Liberty Song" (originally
published in the *Boston Gazette,* and sung by the Sons of Liberty); "The
World Turned Upside Down," the piece of music sometimes said to have
been played (but not authenticated) at Cornwallis' surrender; "The
Death of Warren" and "Bunker Hill," "Cornwallis Burgoynes," and

many others. Note that all the arrangements of songs used on these records are copyrighted.

COSTUMES

To find out how soldiers and citizens dressed in Revolutionary days, you can consult several sources: paintings of the period, the Library of Congress, the Smithsonian Institution, historical societies, and books, both old and new.

BOOKS AND PICTURES

Half the fun and the benefit resulting from putting on a dramatic presentation is the assembling of the costumes. Most of these advantages come from creating the costumes themselves. As already noted, civilian costumes, both male and female (gentry, workers, tradespeople, children's clothes, and even some military clothes) are comparatively easy to make, which is certainly less expensive than renting them. In any case, the underwear and the accessories—so important to authenticity and style—must be homemade, or at least drastically altered. In addition, costumes designed and made for specific shows guarantee that the colors not only harmonize but set the mood for specific scenes.

The sketches in Part V, The First Rehearsal, show how costumes can be made from modern, relatively inexpensive materials. Consult these sketches!

For further suggestions, there are innumerable pictures by contemporary artists that are available as models for costumes, makeup, hairdos, and all other details. The best of these illustrations are by Trumbull, Gilbert Stuart, Charles Willson Peale, and Benjamin West, copies of whose works should be in your local library or in the library of your art school, college, high school, or university. Besides, most of the histories listed above have excellent reproductions of contemporary cartoons and line drawings. Additional copies can be had by writing to:

The Department of prints
  Congressional Library
  Washington, D.C.

The Colonial Costume Department
  Smithsonian Institution
  Washington, D.C.

The Mount Vernon Ladies Association
  Mount Vernon
  Virginia

Books for young people that contain detailed line sketches easy to follow are:

Washington's America, Robin McKown (Grosset & Dunlap)
Boys in the Revolution, Jack Coggins (Stackpole)

Pictures of Revolutionary notables like Washington, Jefferson, Franklin, Adams, and so on, are easy to come by almost anywhere, and, of course, their clothes can be used as a basis for making other clothes, with slight variations of accessories or color. Also, you will need these pictures as a basis for makeup.

MILITARY COSTUMES

The Revolution was half over by the time the United States Army uniform was even partially standardized. The people who fought with Washington, both men and women, enlisted, more often than not, for a few months or a year. They were the ordinary farmers, working people, and tradespeople, and they brought their own equipment, like sidearms, pots and pans, and bedding rolls, with them, and were either given only parts of uniforms or just a cockade or a chevron. Therefore, any book that has pictures of uniforms of the Continental soldiers is useful for detailed drawings of shoes, cuffs, stocks and handkerchiefs, leggings, belts, eyeglasses, hand lanterns, bottles, and almost everything you can name.

The Picture Book of the Continental Soldier, Keith Wilbur (Stackpole), has a page on how to dress a man's hair.

The Book of the Continental Soldier, Harold L. Peterson (Stackpole), is full of fine details; especially helpful are contemporary drawings made on the spot.

The uniforms of the Navy were even more haphazard. For this subject, see *Ships and Seamen of the American Revolution,* Jack Coggins (Stackpole).

RENTALS

In case there are a few especially elaborate costumes that you feel you must rent, explore your local facilities before doing anything else. Compare what is available with your authentic pictures. Be careful about mixing fabrics and ornamentation, except for emphasis. If your homemade men's costumes, for instance, are made of painted canvas, be careful about introducing real velvet costumes into the same scene unless you want to make a contrast between rich and poor, or a private with a general. A real brocade dress on a lady will make her stand out in a scene where most of the women are dressed in cotton or painted costumes. Real gold braid shows up in the midst of modern soutache. Whenever and wherever you rent a costume, be sure to get written permission to alter or make any changes whatsoever.

If you need a large number of costumes like an authentic military company, you will have to go to the theatrical centers to get them. East of the Mississippi, there are: Brooks Van Horn, 16 West 61st Street, New York, N.Y. and Eaves Costume Company, 151 West 46th Street, New York, N.Y. For west of the Mississippi, contact: Western Costume Company, Hollywood, California.

Although these companies are generally reliable, it is preferable to have somebody you trust go to their warehouse and select and check the costumes before they are sent.

If you have no one of your own to do this, a good place to get in touch with is: Theatre Production Service, 54 Fourth Avenue, New York, N.Y. They will go shopping for you for almost anything—costumes, sound equipment, light equipment, artifacts, and even animals and directors.

Be sure that rented costumes are sent you in plenty of time for you to alter them or even exchange them if they are not satisfactory. Be sure to put this condition into your contract with any rental company. Don't forget insurance and be sure to find out whether the price quoted includes shipping, packing, and insurance.

WEAPONS AND HARDWARE

Sidearms—guns, swords, pistols, knives—are supposed to come with rented costumes, as are belts, but not shoes. Fortunately, shoes that are in style today with their rounded toes and low heels can easily be transformed into Colonial shoes by the addition of buckles, bows, etc. But the question of how to get arms must be solved locally. Perhaps there is a historical museum which will lend you such items, or an advertisement in the paper may turn up a collector. Once more, don't forget insurance.

The Journal of the American Revolution, published by the Brigade of the American Revolution, 2411 Olive Street, Philadelphia, Pa. 19130, carries advertisements of artifacts for sale.

COSTUMED GROUPS

You may be surprised to hear it but all over the place people have been meeting for years in companies, in troupes, and just plain clubs, dressing themselves in Colonial costumes, and studying and dramatizing different phases of our history. There may be such a group near you that you can use. They have their own costumes and many of them have artifacts and hardware. Some of them are professionals, like those at Williamsburg and Sturbridge, Massachusetts, but many of them just do it as a hobby. Most of these contingents have developed set presentations. When you invite them to participate, be sure they understand that you are going to use them in the same way that we have already described in the section on returning local celebrities. You must not stop your dramatic presentation in the middle while a troupe does a manual of arms that they have practiced—unless it might be a scene at Valley Forge with Baron von Steuben drilling Washington's troops.

If you live near Baltimore or Philadelphia, the very elegant Maryland Fifth Regiment or the Philadelphia Horse Troop might lend some glamor. At Fort Myers, Virginia, the First Company of the Third Army is especially prepared to take part in celebrations.

Among such hobby groups, one of the largest, with many chapters, is The Brigade of the American Revolution, 2411 Olive Street, Philadelphia, Pa. 19130. Other addresses from which performing groups may be obtained are The Company of Fifers and Drummers, c/o David Beddie, 2049 34th Street, S.E., Washington, D.C., and Registrar, Company of Fifers and Drummers, 16 Winter Avenue, Deep River, Conn. Both of these organizations have chapters scattered all over. The Brigade even has one as far from the original thirteen states as Oregon. Both also put out publications. In the Brigade's *Journal of the American Revolution,* for instance, there is not only a list of their membership but advertisements telling where to get things, and authentic sketches and pictures of Colonial uniforms and artifacts, and where to buy them. There is nothing like a good, well-trained troop of fifers and drummers to liven up your music score.

One group needs special mention. It is the marvellous Fanfare Group, with beautiful, long, silver trumpets and trombones, copies of instruments designed for the Director of Music of the British Army in 1932. The music for the group is also specially written for it. The name and address is:

Valley Forge Military Academy Fanfare Group,
Colonel D. Keith Feltham, Conductor,
Valley Forge Military Academy, Wayne, Pa. 19087.

Let me repeat my warning. When inviting these groups, be specific about the part you want them to play in your pageant.

LIGHTING AND SOUND, MULTIMEDIA, TECHNICAL EQUIPMENT, ETC.

Most of your technical equipment can probably be borrowed from TV stations and Little Theaters, public playgrounds, and stadiums in your own area. However, if you do need special equipment, the best and most reliable places to get them are:

Century Lighting Company, 3 Entin Road, Clifton, N.J.
Kleigl-Universal, 3232 48th Ave., Long Island City, N.Y.

These companies have branches in other places.

Write to Simon's Directory, c/o Package Publicity Service, 1564 Broadway, New York, N.Y. 10036 for a large volume, containing hundreds of addresses where you can rent almost anything, technical or otherwise, that you may need. This directory is used widely, though commercially, by little theaters, universities, and other producing groups almost everywhere, and has a good reputation for accuracy. The introduction is written by Jo Mielziner, the distinguished producer-designer.

Multimedia material is, no doubt, already being used by your local school teachers and university professors in their classes. Ask them about it. Also inquire whether your own TV or radio station or utility company has any appropriate film clips, motion pictures, tapes, or recordings on file.

Most of these things can be rented (not cheap) or bought (even more expensive). Send for catalogues to either of the following addresses:

Texfilm Division, McGraw Hill Company,
   330 West 42nd Street, New York, N.Y.   10036
Colonial Williamsburg, Film Distribution Section,
   Drawer C, Williamsburg, Va.   23185

BACKSTAGE MANAGEMENT

A *must* for the proper conduct of backstage deportment is the following book: *The Stage Manager's Handbook,* by Bert Gruver, published by Drama Book Store Publications, Inc., 15 West 52nd Street, New York, N.Y.

PUBLICITY

The Package Publicity Service, 1564 Broadway, New York, N.Y. 10036, supplies publicity kits for community theaters throughout the country. You may wish to make use of some of their suggestions.

RESTORATIONS AND DEDICATIONS

There are nationwide organizations, privately financed, whose object is to hunt out landmarks worthy of preservation. However, in your research you may find something in your own locale that has been overlooked. You may be able to get one of these organizations to designate your spot as a historic landmark.

The principal sources for information about spots already designated, and how and where to put pressure on for your site which may have been overlooked, are:

The National Trust Fund for Historic Preservations,
748 Jackson Place, N.W., Washington, D.C. 20006.

The National Audubon Society,
1130 Fifth Avenue, New York, N.Y. 10028.

The Sierra Club,
225 Bush Street, San Francisco, Calif.

Sites already on the published list of the first organization above include places not only in the thirteen original states but in the old Northwest Territory, in the Southwest, and on the Coast. These last two are especially interested in preservation and rehabilitation of the ecology. Who knows, there may be some natural phenomenon in your neighborhood, like a Washington elm or a wildlife preserve worthy of dedication, which has been overlooked. This aspect of the restoration of the environment is one of the chief targets of the National Commission on the American Revolution.

OFFICIAL AND GENERAL

Excellent brochures containing specific information and broad guidelines in almost every aspect of the Bicentennial Celebration are being issued officially by government departments and especially appointed commissions, whose business it is to promote the Bicentennial. Many states, and even cities, have appointed such commissions. If there is one in your area, be sure to contact it. If you can't find out who they are, you can write to the National Commission.

There is a perfect storehouse of ideas and suggestions, among them such titles as "Themes Deserving Emphasis," "Namesake City Celebrations," and "Historic Sites in the National Park System," contained in

The Report of the Secretary of the Interior to the American Revolution Bicentennial Commission, available from the Superintendent of Documents, U.S. Government Printing Office, Washington, D.C. 20240 (price: 55¢). And above all, communicate freely with The National Park Service of the Department of the Interior, Harper's Ferry, Va., or c/o Department of the Interior, Washington, D.C. 20240, and the Executive Director, the American Revolution Bicentennial Commission, 763 Jackson Place, N.W., Washington, D.C. 20076.